IT'S IN YOUR BLOOD!
"GENETICS OR EXCUSES?"

MAKING THE TRANSFORMATION FROM A BOY TO A MAN...

JOHNTA KNIGHT

authorHOUSE®

AuthorHouse™
1663 Liberty Drive
Bloomington, IN 47403
www.authorhouse.com
Phone: 1-800-839-8640

First published by AuthorHouse 06/22/2011

ISBN: 978-1-4567-6007-6 (sc)
ISBN: 978-1-4567-6006-9 (dj)
ISBN: 978-1-4567-6005-2 (e)

Library of Congress Control Number: 2011905205

Printed in the United States of America

Table of Contents

Part 1: Love Built on a Flawed Foundation

Part 2: My Story

Part 3: Transitioning from a Boy to a Man: The Spiritual Realm

Introduction:
Getting to Know That Person in the Mirror

The common man from all walks of life will establish several different types of relationships along the way. From personal to business relationships, a man has to make the best decisions for himself. In this book, I'll focus more on the man's responsibilities. The transitional stage is vital. The only way a boy makes the full transformation is by learning from a man or men who have made the full transformation themselves. It's sad that we have a lot of grown boys in this world, and I can honestly say I was one myself.

Manhood begins with the spirit. If you're right in the spiritual realm, then you will make the right decisions, regardless of the situation. Man's sinful nature is a tough thing to deal with. Most sin has an addictive nature about it, whether it is lying, alcoholism, or fornication. If we are consistently acting in a sinful manner, we will develop a habit or addiction to that sin. This will continue unless we replace our bad habits with good ones and deny our flesh the pleasures of the world. The Bible speaks of the *generational curse*. This is when people suffer for the sins of their parents or their ancestors. It has little to do with individual salvation or spiritual destiny—or does it? Deuteronomy 24:16 of the (KJV) King James Version "The fathers shall not be put to death for the children, neither shall the children be put to death for the fathers: every man shall be put to death for his own sin.

Then there's Exodus 34:7 of the (KJV) Keeping mercy for thousands, forgiving iniquity and transgression and sin, and by no means clear the guilty; visiting the iniquity of the fathers upon the children, and upon the children's children, unto the third and to the forth generation. Personally, when I first read this, my perception of this Scripture was misconstrued. Look closely at the part that states, **"He punishes the children and their children for the sin of their fathers to the third and fourth generation."** If my father sin, he will be punished for only his sins. If I commit the same sins as my father, my evil deeds shall not go unpunished, but only I will answer to God for my indiscretions. It's only a generational curse if my father, son, and I commit the same sin, voiding God's commands.

What do I mean when using the phrase, "it's in your blood"? Let's start with *genetics*, the branch of biology that deals with heredity and genetic variations. *Heredity* is the passing on of genetic factors, such as hair color or flower color, from one generation to the next in living organisms. "It's in your blood," is only part of the book's title. What exactly do I mean when I say *excuses*? My definition of an excuse is a false reason that enables somebody to do something they want to do or avoid something they don't want to do. Most men wrestle with themselves the majority of their lives trying to pin down their identities. This could be a great thing in terms of a progressive career (excelling in a career of choice and enjoying what it is that you do), or it could lead to a miserably stressful life because of the countless blunders it causes (costly mistakes made over and over again, normally resulting in an extremely difficult lifestyle). It's impractical to have a different outcome when using the same approach. Several questions surface over time: How do I become a better man? How do I become a better husband? How do I become a better father? How do I become a better friend? How do I become a better person altogether?

From what I've witnessed along the paths I've traveled in my life, women usually know what they want. Unfortunately, the majority of men spend half their lives trying to find themselves. A man without direction is lost in every aspect of his life, which results in men finding themselves all over the place. Does this sound familiar? Play or be played—you can't help it; it's in your blood! That's where the million-dollar question comes in to play: is it genetics or excuses? Some may even say it's a little bit of both. Here, my life is an open book; see where I've been, where I am, and where I'm going. Hopefully you will take something from it. But whatever you do, share it with someone else.

Preface

Acceptance

I truly believe the first step toward manhood is acceptance, and wisdom will soon follow. For starters, be realistic with the one person you cannot fool: yourself. Speaking from personal experiences, I chose to live most of my adulthood drowning in a pool of lies. Once you tell one lie, you have to continue to tell even more lies to cover all of the ones you've told in the past. You've now become selfish and capricious. You begin to not only act on impulse, but you also become cancerous to those who love you. You eventually create a burden in your fictitious world that will become unbearable to carry. The same pain you give to so many, comes to you. In other words, what goes around comes around.

I've struggled with many of these issues, and it is from a place of personal experience and wisdom through trial and error that I divulge this information to you. I became whoever I needed to be at any given time in order to get whatever I wanted. But in this equation, I never factored in what the consequences would be for my actions. Every action has a reaction, and repercussions come with karma. You allow yourself to go so far with lies, you begin to add even more weight to the burden you already carry. That added stress makes you want to tell the truth, but you can't, because that would expose you for who you really are. Unfortunately for you at this stage, it is only in truth that freedom can be found. Trust me; this is a burden you don't want to carry. In taking another step toward manhood, you have to accept responsibility. If you put yourself in any situation, good or bad, take full responsibility for your actions at all times. As a father of five, a husband, brother, and uncle, I have quite the task ahead of me. The only way to set a good example and leave a lasting impression is to walk a righteous path. I'm responsible for all the eyes that have been placed upon me. Therefore, I have to be the best husband, father, brother, and uncle I can be. I can only expect from others what I'm willing to give.

For all those boys trapped in men's bodies, the fountain of youth is not fictitious. The fountain of youth is not found in some special water, in a younger woman, or in a sports car. The fountain of youth is in the bloodline; its genetics. It's in our children. Die for yourself, but live for and through your children. Accept responsibility, and be a great father. To take another step toward manhood, you have to be aware of and accept change. Don't resist, because change is constant; you must learn to adjust. Remember that making the transition from a boy to a man begins with acceptance.

The Discovery

I was told that my penis would make me a slave if I let it. After revisiting the same mistakes countless times, I realized that it wasn't my penis that made me a slave to hardship. The bad decisions we make are what cause the consequences we experience. I chose to emulate male figures close to me, and they gave me the same bad information they received. It's a vicious cycle!

Proverbs 1:7 (KJV) "The fear of the Lord is the beginning of knowledge; but fools despise wisdom and instruction." Once a child retains bad information from the lips of a fool, it's like placing a virus into a database. Once we're at the age when we truly understand right and wrong, we have to seek knowledge ourselves. This is when the real journey begins.

The Sponge

This is my version of a man welcoming his son into the world: Curiosity starts from birth, and anxiety for the parents starts as soon as the child leaves the hospital. The journey home becomes nerve-wracking for the parents and quite the adventure for the child. "Hello, son!" These are the words from a proud father welcoming his child into this brutal world. At this point, your son has no idea how cruel the world can be. He does not have any worries. By three months, he has come a long way. Now that he's able to hold his head up, you can see progress. The baby boy is resilient, and he no longer wants to sleep all of the time. He's starting to become aware of things around him. After just two months in the world, he attempts to hold his own bottle. He's beginning to taste independence. There's no way you want to hold this youngster back! He's curious about everything. He begins to crawl, and before you know it, he'll be walking. You place him in his walker, and he takes off before you remove your hands from beneath his arms. What is this? That's what he's asking. Of course, he's speaking another language—baby talk. Although you can't make out what he is saying, he understands you just fine. The next step toward his independence is walking. Shortly after, he will be introduced to the potty. He will wonder, *What is this cool toy? Water comes out of it.* He plays with it like a toy. Having no idea what it is, he learns the responsibility that comes with his discovery over time. This is just the beginning! One day his innocence will diminish, especially if the right examples aren't set for him and if he's not taught to keep God's commands.

Finally, your son is out of the walker stage, and no matter how long you keep him in that swing, he refuses to fall asleep! Oh, no! That's right, at this stage he wants to know what's going on around him at all times. He's thirsty for knowledge. You have the opportunity to mold his mind before the world takes a crack at it. You're probably thinking he's just a baby. Wrong! He's a little person with a sponge for a mind, and he's ready to absorb anything and everything. I know children have to crawl before they walk, but their minds are always running.

Please note that the statement "product of my environment" is way overrated. I say this because my environment was terrible, but my foundation was rock solid. Caretakers should prepare children for everything that goes on outside the home. It's complicated to do, but it's not impossible. Although I made bad decisions, I thought twice before making them. I'm not attempting to justify anything by saying, "I thought twice about it." All I'm saying is if the right things weren't taught to me growing up, I would have made those bad decisions without a single thought. If you don't take the time to instill the right information in your children, I hope you're not depending on the world to do it for you. If so, expect to be disappointed!

PART 1

Love Built on a Flawed Foundation

Chapter 1
Seven Important Questions to Ask Yourself

I began to write this book with hopes of finding myself. It all started with seven questions. Before you ask yourself these seven questions, I would like you to start by doing this: take the time to think way outside of the box. In order to begin this exercise I need you to get a piece of fruit at this time. What I'm trying to accomplish here may appear to be a little crazy, but it's necessary to reach the point that I'm trying to make. Okay! Are you ready? I'll assume you have an orange in your hand. Remember you have to give yourself your undivided attention! I want you to concentrate on that piece of fruit for as long as it takes to make your mind believe that the orange you are now looking at is yellow. Your response is probably, "What?" Am I right? Well that's what your reflection says to you every time you look into the mirror. It's impossible to lie to yourself! You can fool a lot of people, but at no time will you ever be able to fool yourself. I've tried to fool myself for years, but I'm not buying it! Therefore I came up with an exercise for myself, sort of a checklist. You have to ask yourself one question a day. I would advise you to do this only when there are no distractions. Regardless of whether you are single or married, with or without children, the best time to do this is after taking a shower. I find myself to be more relaxed and focused. If you care to try this, please be my guest. Keep in mind that this isn't a quick exercise. After you get out of the shower or bath, I want you to look that person in the mirror dead in the eye. I want you to ask that person the first question on the list. Remember! You must be able to answer the question not just honestly, but your answer has to be more than satisfying to you. It might take you a lot longer than some, depending on your goals and the height of the success bar that you've set for yourself. If any of your answers are not satisfying to you, make time to work on those areas of displeasure.

Do I Love Myself?

If I were to answer this question based from my actions, I would probably say no! Why is this? When you respect yourself and others, you may also love yourself. I never gave myself a real shot at life. I thought I was "the man" at one point, receiving worthless praises from friends for sleeping with countless women. I was a womanizer, a master at misleading women! What exactly did I get from this? I'll tell you what I got from this: three kids, crabs, and gonorrhea. That's right, sexually transmitted diseases! In the twelfth grade, I was sitting on a friend's porch, having a general conversation about girls. One of my friends started talking about how dirty some of the girls who attended our school were, as if we were any better! He then went on to say that one of the females who attended our school had given him crabs. *What's that?* I thought. He then went on to explain how he discovered them. I never said anything, but I decided to go home that night and look myself over thoroughly. What did I discover? Crabs! I started itching instantly. I was scared to death. A bottle of crab lice shampoo resolved the problem, but this was just the beginning of my self-inflicted pain, the beginning of the "I can't possibly love myself" phase. Crabs didn't mean I was irresponsible, I decided. It had nothing to do with unprotected sex. After telling myself this, I decided to stay in the race. My next prize would be—drum roll please—Gonorrhea! I was told to take fourteen pills: two pills a day for seven days. You think this stopped me? Not a chance. I loved myself too much to take precautions at this point. I continued my quest to greatness, asking myself, "Who will I sleep with next?" With a little persistence, I just might have been able to win genital herpes. I might even have had a shot for higher stakes: HIV. Although there's no cure for herpes, I figured I could control it. Since I loved myself to death, I figured I'd roll the dice until I was diagnosed with AIDS.

Does this sound like the type of game anyone who loves himself would play? I don't think so! But believe it or not, this is the type of game we play with our lives. The stakes are high, and the grand prize is life. Every time you gamble with your life, you're putting someone else's at risk, as well. I had no idea that I was setting the pitch for the rest of my life. I was becoming the same grown boy who had broken my mother's heart countless times. Although my father was not in the picture during a critical phase of my life, it would seem I inherited his bad habits. I began getting women pregnant without a clue of how I was going to take care of them. I loved myself so much I would spend all my teenage years and most of my adulthood risking everything. If you don't love yourself, how can you possibly love anyone else? You can't! I was dating the woman who is now my wife. I was reckless! My only concern was me, me, and me! I took numerous chances of contracting and passing on sexually transmitted diseases to my girlfriend. If I didn't care about myself, why would I be concerned about anyone else's health? It's by the grace of God that my girlfriend during this time later became my wife. She never contracted anything from me, but I most definitely put her in harm's way. I can truly say that I love myself now! What I did then has affected not only me, but my relationship with my wife as well. She has to share me with women whom I wouldn't have anything to do with had I loved myself enough to protect myself. As a result of what I did in the past, those terrible decisions have a negative impact on every aspect of my life. Having to make decisions for my children outside of my marriage has definitely affected my relationship with my wife. Those poor choices that I made as a kid set me up for many years of emotional distress as an adult. How different my life would be if I had only loved myself. Every journey begins with a step. Only you will be held accountable whether you take that step in the right or wrong direction.

Am I Happy at This Point in My Life?

That's a good question! Happiness starts with you! If you're totally unhappy, how is it possible to make someone else happy? This is such a broad question, because no one is always happy, right? I guess that depends on what a person considers being happy. I can say I'm happy when I'm with my wife. She sets the mood for the rest of my day. I'm only unhappy with some of the decisions I have made. Life isn't exactly peaches and cream, but at the same time, you should have more sunny days than cloudy days. Have you ever heard anyone say, "If you fail to prepare, then you are preparing for failure"? That is a very true statement! I've never given myself any real options. I never made arrangements for life after high school. That's how much I prepared myself. I obtained the blueprint for failure even before I became a teenager. As a result, I carried those bad habits into adulthood. There is so much I want to accomplish in life, but a lack of education and determination will not allow me to leave the lobby floor. Sometimes I feel as if I don't have all of the necessary tools to bring success within reach, but I have no one to blame for this but myself. I have so many regrets! It almost feels as if I'm a perplexed archaeologist. Instead of digging for artifacts in the ground, I often feel like I'm in the ground upside down, digging for the sun. Every day above ground is supposed to be a good day. As boys, we make a lot of bad choices, but as men, we live them. Life should be played out like the game of chess and never like the game of checkers. At no time should you make a move without thought.

Do I Enjoy What I Do for a Living?

Although the workplace is considered your livelihood, under no circumstances should you bring work-related frustrations home. I'm not saying you shouldn't be able to talk to your significant other about work-related issues, but know the difference between venting and arguing. *Home should set the tone for work; work should never set the tone for home!* My wife didn't choose my employer; I did! At one point, I would save all my frustrations for home. My wife would meet me at the door with eyes that screamed, "I missed you," and a smile that could brighten anyone's day. I continued to bring work-related aggravations home and take them out on my wife. All she wanted in return was a hug and to stare into a set of eyes that said, "I miss you, too." A woman such as this defines unconditional love. She could care less that I had been sweating all day; the smell was of no importance. She just wanted affection from her husband. Although she loves me now and loved me then, she's only human. Pay attention! What I'm about to show you is how a negative action causes a negative reaction. After so many times of showing her how unappreciative I was and making everything about me and my bad day, she stopped meeting me at the door. Not long after, the venting turned into arguments. Then the communication slowly began to cease.

I had no intention of pushing my wife away. That goes to show you how quickly things can happen. You never miss a great thing until it's gone. We became so distant, all because of how unhappy I was with the type of work I did for a living and with myself.

At no point can you be egocentric once you commit to a person who loves you just as much as you love yourself. You must be aware at all times that what you do affects everyone around you. We often complain about how imperfect our relationships are, and we always seem to forget how we got there. I've learned to be more attentive to my actions, and lucky for me, I have a willing and understanding wife. My wife and I have a great thing, and I'm pleased to say we're back on track. This is just one of many ways your relationship can get off track if you're not careful. I now think before I speak, because words become actions. Actions become habits. Habits become character, and character sets your destiny. Simple things like this can cause bigger problems down the road. Sometimes we get so far down the road that we often forget how to get back to where it all began. Do I enjoy what I do for a living? Not really! Do you? If you did what you really loved doing for a living, would the sun shine more often? Make a list of all of the things that make you unhappy. You might not be able to change them overnight, but with God, effort, and prayer, you can be happy.

Do I Have Any Goals?

The first step toward reaching a goal or goals is having them. Brilliant statement, right? At some point in our lives, we have to realize that when what we know doesn't help us, there's a strong possibility that what we don't know is what's hindering us. Sometimes we put our goals so far in the rear, they almost don't exist. The number one excuse for not pursuing and achieving goals would probably be not having enough time! That's my favorite excuse. It's important that young boys prioritize and create good habits for themselves early on in life. This is one way to eliminate unnecessary hardships once they become men. Once you become complacent with doing just enough to get by, goals that require persistence and hard work usually get scratched off the list of things to do.

I was raised in a cynical environment where the ultimate and only goals to shoot for were, becoming a rap star or a professional athlete.

If neither goal was obtained, we could always depend on the block to hold us down. That's what we called shooting for the stars. We knew so little about being productive. Every one of us thought we could actually major in professional football. No one in our community taught us anything different. The neighborhood is where men are supposed to teach young boys how to become men. We were so young and closed-minded. How were we supposed to know the right questions to ask? Apparently the men around us didn't have the answers. They never set out to earn degrees with the intention of educating themselves or the next generation. This is one of many ways in which what you don't know can hinder you. I had no idea the world was so big, and the possibilities with-in it were endless. I was an adult, a fully grown boy, by the time I realized that life had so much more to offer. I didn't have to be just another statistic or a product of my environment, but by the time I realized this, I had already set up several preventable obstacles that I then had to hurdle in order to achieve my goals. These are the avertable adversities that I speak about. I can honestly say that I'm proud to have accomplished one of many goals; I closed on my first house before age thirty. That might not mean anything to some, and it could mean reaching for the stars for others, but that achievement gave me the clarification I needed, teaching me that achieving goals that appear to be out of reach really can happen. Now I'm starving; I want more! What's next on the list? You're looking at it; I'm done making excuses and dragging my feet. If you are reading this book, I've accomplished yet another goal.

Instead of making excuses, make progress! Most of us have to work while chasing our dreams, but anything worth having is worth working hard for!

Am I Implementing Any Plan to Reach Those Goals?

Reaching goals requires research as well as patience and persistence. You cannot get around the two "p" words; I would probably say that they are the two main ingredients for success. In order to finish this book, I had to work extremely hard. I had to work around long hours at work, spending time with my wife and kids, and being fatigued. When you have a passion for anything in life, you will turn a twenty-four-hour day into twenty-eight hours. In other words, you will make time! Passion is something that you absolutely have to have!

My first quest was to read more. Reading strengthens your vocabulary, and writing is my passion as well as my craft. My eyes push up on words, and I can feel my mind getting strong! Books are like weight bars, and the words inside them are the weights. Your mind is the muscle that grows depending on how much you work out. After I realized that, I had to prioritize! This meant that I had to sacrifice something I love in order to do what I love. Did I lose you just then? I love to watch TV, but if I plan on writing books for a living, I have to watch less TV and do more reading and writing. I had to write at least one page a day—no exceptions. I was given a book called *Writer's Market*, and that's probably the best gift my father-in-law could have ever given me. It helped me to identify my work with those who would be interested in the type of material I write. This kept me from wasting a lot of time trying to find my market. I also had to research publishers. Without a publisher, all I would have is a manuscript. I pursued music before, and I failed according to my own standards. Although I didn't break into the industry, I have the satisfaction of knowing that I chased that dream for a really long time. I was writing raps, but nevertheless, I was writing. I've been writing poems since the eighth grade, and I've realized that writing is something I have to do. Not accomplishing something while in pursuit is not considered failure—just a delay! It becomes failure once you give up on it.

According to Me, Are My Priorities in Order?

For those fortunate enough to have their lives planned out for them and smart enough to stay on course, good job! When you are disciplined enough to do what you must before you do what you want, you are well on your way to becoming a responsible person. Prioritizing is all about being responsible. If you're not responsible, how can your priorities be in order? I know I say "according to me," but let's be real about it. Are my priorities in order if I take care of my home first? This question is for those of you who are like me. At one point, I used to listen to stupid remarks; I was a follower. I was far from the leader I appeared to be when I looked in the mirror. Men who were supposedly grown quoted to me, "As long as you take care of your home first, you're handling your business." What a joke! I actually believed that at one time. If it makes sense to you, then you're in for a big surprise. If you think your priorities are in order, just wait until your infidelities catch up with you. Believe me, they always do! A guy about sixty years of age whom I work with shared something with me out of the blue. We were talking about why men have to sleep with so many women. He said, "I always take care of home first!" He's on marriage number two. I understand that no one is perfect, and we all have our hang-ups, but at what point do we grow up? When do we make the final transformation from a boy to a man? I said, "Is that why you work so much? So you can have money to run the streets after you pay the bills at home?"

"You think I enjoy working all the time? I have no choice," he replied.

I responded, "What do you mean?"

"Man, I have children who are only four months and seven years old, by two women outside of my marriage," he replied. I was definitely not expecting that: wow!

I then replied, "So you're paying money outside your household to women just to keep this a secret. I know you're miserable!" This is one example of how deceitfulness can cause you a lifetime of pain. This irresponsible act is devastating for the children born out of wedlock! I feel for them, because they had nothing to do with this negligent act. This is the behavior of a sixty-year-old boy who calls himself a man. Who can the youth really look up to? I have had to change my ways because I have a wife, daughters, and sons. What example would I be setting if I continued to surf through life with such a reckless approach? I'm far from a saint, but I can now say that according to me, I'm doing just fine. We all have a past. Change comes with challenges and accountability. I used to have that same mentality, thinking that as long as I take care of my home first, I'm fine. Now I only take care of home!

Am I Satisfied?

Well, are you? I can say that I'm far from it! I'm thirsty for change! I'm thankful, but very unsatisfied. Maybe it's just me, but I feel when people say they are satisfied, they're settling. I have too much to learn, too many places I want to see, and too many things I would like to accomplish before I can say that I'm content. I can truly say that God is good! I'm blessed two times over, but far from satisfied! I would like to see some of my work performed on the big stage someday. I would love to work with Tyler Perry, I admire his art, it has a lot of substance. I've had the opportunity to see his work performed live, and it makes me appreciate the art. I believe that with anything you do in your lifetime, someone before you has attempted or has done it. You should read up on people you aspire to be like. How did he accomplish so much? What or who inspired her to overcome the many obstacles that stood on her path? How did he prevail in the face of adversity? What was she thinking when she wrote that novel? What was he thinking when he wrote that play? What made her give up stability for possibilities? How did he know to step out on faith? I have so many questions and so much I need to learn. I believe that anyone who loves something will master their craft, no matter what it is. I feel that the only way to master something is to be patient, humble, persistent, and, above all, obedient to the ways of God. Am I satisfied? I'm a starving artist; my stomach is touching my back! The only thing that can fill my stomach is passion, the passion I have for my craft.

Chapter 2
In Search for the Balance

Does the background a man comes from really dictate the type of man he will become? Do the male figures around him really play a part in the way he views women? I often feel like a little boy trapped in a grown man's frame. I constantly make the same mistakes as a child would. Transforming from a boy to a man can be quite difficult for some. Making this transition has everything to do with the type of male figure one chooses to emulate. I chose to use the term "male figure" instead of "man," simply because every boy does not grow up! What do I mean by this? All boys are considered men once they are of age, but many of our actions reflect those of a child.

How can a man remain monogamous if he's taught to never fully trust any woman, not even his own mother? I believe that there are positive and negative influences, and there always will be. I also believe in choices; every man makes the best decision for himself. Take it from me: the main ingredient in a boy's upbringing is reality. For example, if your son is fascinated with a pimp, he needs to be educated on the downside of that type of lifestyle. Either you can allow him to get the glamorous side only from someone else, or you can shed some light on the subject yourself. I personally have a friend whose father is a pastor. He is a well-rounded person, but he was sheltered. He was a student athlete and received an academic and athletic scholarship. Instead of excelling at Penn State, the school of his choice, he ended up in the state penitentiary. Why is that? He didn't want to be like his father. He chose instant gratification. His father might have done everything right, but in the end, a boy who thinks he's a man makes the final decision. Many of us hate to admit that we are just grown boys with no real intentions of ever growing up.

The first step to becoming a man would probably be better decision making. It seems that we're always on the go. That's one of the bigger issues when it comes to our relationships. Most of us feel like we can't win when it comes to balancing our relationships and time. It seems that when we chase money, we lack time, and as a result, we leave our significant other upset. Most of us do not have the luxury of staying at home. Most men's mentality is, "If we don't put in hours, we don't get paid!" If we give her time and no money, she makes an extreme transformation from whispering sweet nothings into our ears to nothing at all. It takes a continuous effort on both ends to make things work. It's imperative that you find the balance. The number one question for more than half of America would probably be, "How do I make everyone happy?" I can counterpunch that question and follow up with one even better. First let me start by saying that it's easy to make everyone who plays an important role in your life happy at some point. The real question is how do you keep everyone happy? Now that's a tough one! Is this even possible? I believe we all have somewhat similar but generally very different lifestyles. I guess it's safe to say that though we all live on the same planet, we live in utterly different worlds. A certain level of responsibility and expectation are placed upon each and every one of us. In some cases, the liabilities we bear result from poor decisions. Just like most, I would scream out, "There's not enough time in a day!" It sometimes seems impossible to balance my time between my wife and others. This book is all about prioritizing!

Whether you know it or not, there is a way to keep your relationships bearable. I like to call it the order of love. In the Bible, that same message is relayed to each and every one of us. The Bible talks about how a man should love his wife just as God loves the church. It speaks of the importance of having a relationship with God, your wife, your children, and so forth. Love is like algebra; knowing the order of operations is vital. When you are trying to come up with the solution, you can't go wrong if you follow the order of operations. All you have to remember is who comes first. Your next step is to plug everyone and everything else in accordingly. Life is like a puzzle. As long as the pieces are there, you will always have a chance to put them together. We begin to pick up pieces from birth, if we are fortunate. Although some of us are getting the pieces we need to complete the puzzle our entire lives, we begin to lose them in time. We often take life for granted. Many of us aren't as fortunate, so we have to go out and obtain the pieces ourselves. Nevertheless, this makes the puzzle much more meaningful once it's finished. Let me be the first to say that I've most definitely taken my life for granted. I'm now trying to gather all of the right pieces with the hope of seeing the big picture one day. I'm trying to make the transformation from a boy to a man in every aspect of my life. In this book, I've focused on several different aspects of life. I was told that if there's nothing going on in your life, more than likely, you're experiencing the quiet before the storm. When it seems that nothing is going right in your life, you're probably in the eye of the hurricane. If you weather the storm and stand strong, you will see the rainbow. My childhood represents the hurricane before it reaches a large body of water. My life today is something like every unfortunate object that just so happened to be in the hurricane's path.

"All over the place" would be one of many ways to describe most men in America. From young lads, we begin our quest for our identities. It's trial and error with most men. The majority, though not all, change numerous times before identifying themselves. It's sad to say: most of the men I know personally never seem to find themselves. As a result, they became grown boys and never made that complete transformation.

Even as an adult, you can find yourself trying to live up to other people's expectations. True happiness comes from within, not from actions taken based on the outside looking in. I found this to be very true. One of the major ingredients for success is patience. Life is a process! At the age of twenty, I was completely lost, so I would act on my frustrations. I was very impatient. I had two children out of wedlock and nothing but time on my hands. If I could turn back the hands of time and be given a second chance with the same way of thinking, I would surely blow it twice. Without a plan, you have nothing! Instant gratification without preparation leaves room for devastation. As young men, our testosterone is high, and our values are extremely low. When your thought process continues to lead you to a dead end, you have to change your way of thinking in order to progress. I found myself in the back of a police car with an arresting officer who was one of my teammates from high school. He was completely discombobulated. He couldn't believe that I, of all people, would do such things. After I was released from jail, I dreaded facing everyone who knew me, but my biggest fear was facing myself. What will the man in the mirror say to me? He had such high expectations for me. Once I arrived home that night, I went to bed unable to hold my head up. It was extremely heavy from disgrace. I was so embarrassed! I just wanted to fly away! There's only one problem: no matter how far I go or how long I run, I could never leave that person in the mirror behind. I took a shower that morning and then proceeded to dry off. Once I began to make my way toward the mirror, I would quickly drop my head. My conscious began to speak aloud, "Look at me!" After brushing my teeth, I finally wiped away the smog that lay heavily upon the mirror. I looked that person facing me in the mirror square in the eyes. No matter how long I stared at him, I just couldn't make out his face. Who is this guy?

How important is making good decisions, prioritizing, and creating good habits? I can tell you firsthand that freedom is a privilege! I believe that early childhood mistakes have the potential to evolve into adulthood catastrophes. So not only is it important that we receive good information, but it's also just as imperative that we share it.

Growing up, who was considered the man in my neighborhood? You were the man if you possessed the nicest car, the most money, and the hottest woman on your arm. I ate it up like candy, the sweet taste of sin! My first mistake was that I chose to emulate the hustler. I'm not focusing on the product, just the way he treats his women. I say women, because I've never met anyone in the streets who was monogamous. I could have probably chosen to emulate the pastor, or the honest, hardworking family man, but I rarely saw those male figures. I only saw the pastor on Sundays. Out of thirty of us young hardheads in the hood, there were only three or four fathers in the home. Although there weren't many fathers around, including my own, my uncles were married. They also had a problem remaining monogamous, however, and their infidelities resulted in divorce papers. They all had wives and girlfriends with benefits. Not all, but most of them have children all over the place. A few have even been married more then once. My question to them was, "Why can't you guys be with one woman?" Believe it or not, none of them could really answer the question. I expected all of them to say that the reason they cheated had something to do with their suspicious and nagging wives. I was right! It's always the woman's fault. "She keeps pushing me out there!" "The answer to everything once she's mad at me is no sex." "What does she think? I'll show her!" It's this way of thinking that causes us to fail each and every time. We never look at ourselves and get to the core of the problem. We should ask ourselves, "Why is she really mad?" I've also been guilty of this ten times over. If your wife is being fair and has substantial reasons for being upset, she has every right to react any way she sees fit. As long as she's not getting violent, you have to do whatever it takes to fix things—on her time, not yours. I've been in this predicament several times. This type of situation is familiar grounds for me. I would get upset once my wife caught me up in something. Then I would turn the tables around, making it about me. I didn't care that I was the one to cause the pain from being deceitful. I would make everything about her, trying to claim it was her fault! *We're not having enough sex,* a man might think, but why is this? Not one male figure would admit that he's at fault. Every action has a reaction! A negative action brings on a negative reaction. Maybe if you take a different approach, you'll get better results. It all starts with you. But after that, it still takes two!

Chapter 3
Never Anchor!

What do I mean when I say, "never anchor?" Under no circumstances should either party settle in. Whatever you did to get your wife's attention, you must do to keep her attention. Whatever you did to make that person fall in love with you, you must continue to do to keep her in love with you. You should never feel like you have a person's heart and therefore find yourself saying, "She's not going anywhere!" Once you begin to feel this way, you will notice that the scenery doesn't change anymore. What happened? You anchored! Sometimes her body might be on board, but I can assure you her heart got off at the last port. Life is short. If you really love the person you're with, please enjoy the journey. Never anchor! Trust is one way to avoid anchoring, remaining monogamous. Do your reasons for being faithful begin with "I love her"? If not, there might be a slight problem. Love should be the only reason you choose to be exclusive with a person. You're with that person simply because you love her unconditionally. Once two people are attracted to one another, the journey begins. They set sail with hopes of having a never ending adventure with limitless possibilities! The journey is a process, since we all know that every journey begins with a step. Nevertheless the direction in which your first step is made is entirely up to you. Although women are usually co-captains, they're more than capable of being the captain of the ship. Behind every good man is an inspiring, strong woman. She not only allows but also wants her captain to navigate the ship. She comes aboard with trust, expectations, and unconditional love. She believes in him. Once her man sets sail, there won't be a port in sight. Although marriage is the destination, that's just the ending of the beginning of the quest. We seem to always think we have the answers to everything, but if that were the case, life would be so simple. Once you reach a point in your relationship where you begin to feel you don't have to listen to your significant other, I can guarantee your journey will be short-lived. You have to keep it real at all times from the beginning to the end.

Is it possible for an imperfect person to find the perfect person? Knowing that perfection doesn't exist, why do we expect it from others? Why do we put so much unnecessary distress on our relationships? Why is it that we expect so much more than we are willing to give? My wife does so much, yet I found myself expecting so much more. A relationship can be simple or complicated. I've learned that a smart person picks and chooses his battles wisely. I'm far from perfect, but I would point out the rare mistakes my wife made. You should never discredit a person, especially when that person is always on top of things. Could it be that I unconsciously seek imperfection in others? I feel as if I do this to make myself feel better about the mistakes I make. People like me want to be right even when we are wrong. We pick and choose our battles very poorly the majority of the time. A relationship is only as strong as the people in it. Even the strongest person gets tired of arguing. Before you bring up an argument to try to prove a point, ask yourself these questions: Is this even worth bringing up? Do I have a valid point? Will anything be resolved? If the answer is no to all three questions, you most definitely shouldn't entertain the thought. Long journeys through life are taken by two understanding and unselfish people. Relationships usually end because of miscommunication. Remember, you can't always be right, and you have to stop looking for what you are far from—perfect! In time, we all will find something we don't like about our significant others, but we have to understand that there are some things they don't like about us. Working on these issues and through them is what makes our relationships so perfect.

Chapter 4
One Mile at a Time

Core Values

What does the phrase "core values" mean to you? Religion, wants, and needs are all considered some of your core values. If two people's beliefs are heading in two completely different directions, how can they coexist? If one has no sense of urgency, and the other party has set out to accomplish great things, how can they coexist? For example, let's say you want a house, but your significant other just wants to rent. What's the happy medium? Let's say you are responsible and you have good credit, but your significant other's credit is shot. How can you progress together? More than likely, one of you will have to pick up the slack for the other. This can get old fast! Kellen and I started dating when we were very young. We had completely different upbringings. The things we both share are resiliency and urgency. We have to look past the obstacles of today in order to obtain the fruits of the future.

Windshield

A windshield to you refers to the glass in the front of your car, but here it represents your future. While traveling in a relationship, you have to see where you are going. While traveling on this road you will encounter several obstacles, one of which I like to call "bugs." Here bugs represent people who are all in your business. If you disclose information with people outside of your relationship, your chances of seeing your future clearly are slim to none.

Windshield Wipers

Windshield Wipers are used to make things clear for you while traveling in a car, but here they represent the strengths of each individual in the relationship. In this case, they are used to see your future more clearly. If you don't wipe away the bugs, eventually they will smear all over your windshield, not allowing you to see or prepare for what's in front of you.

Bumps in the Road and the Wheels of Time

You will hit bumps in the road, and, if you're not careful, you just might hit a pothole. The more you allow people to prey on your relationship, the more tread you lose on the wheels of time. The wheels represent the structure of the relationship. If you don't have good tires on your car, there's a strong possibility that you won't be traveling too far. In order to rest assured, you have to be able to trust your significant other. What do I mean by this? She trusts that you will not do anything to hurt her, and you most defiantly will not pick up any hitchhikers along the way. In other words, she trusts that you won't be bringing any sexually transmitted diseases along for the ride. It's no fun for the person who assumed they were in an exclusive relationship. Once you are married, inappropriate relationships should not exist. This is one sure way to run out of gas. That's why you have to take it one mile at a time. Otherwise, you may find that instead of working through your problems with your significant other, you begin to seek comfort from other members of the opposite sex.

At one point, I found myself having several inappropriate relationships while married. "Blind by choice" is when we choose not to see the other person's intentions. She's never honest with you; she just agrees with you. She is biased because she hopes to gain something. What could a single person really want from a married person? Nothing! Although she knows this already, it all boils down to there being no strings attached. I know this because I've been on the other side, where I was the single one. Inappropriate relationships are inevitable: you cannot have the right ending with the wrong beginning. Speaking from the married man's point of view, are we really that oblivious, or do we intentionally ignore the signs? By doing this, we prepare our consciences to keep us from feeling guilty about our wrongdoing. I've been so dishonest in my life that not telling the truth was normal for me. It was a bad habit that had become a pattern. I couldn't see past my own ego; therefore I couldn't see how fortunate I was. I couldn't see how much my wife loved me. How would I feel if she talked about our problems to a guy that she views as just a friend? You know the type of friend that you have been to a female, the kind of friend that listens very well. Would that be okay with you? Avoidable situations like this leave the door open for Murphy's Law: what can happen, will happen!

In the Driver's Seat

Being in the driver's seat means taking responsibility for the precious cargo that you have aboard. I am a husband and a father; therefore I'm responsible for several lives. I have to drive responsibly in order to assure a safe trip. If I was to continue to drive recklessly, not only could I lose my life, but I would also be putting those who trust me in jeopardy.

How to Please Everyone

Pleasing everyone begins with you. I'm not saying that you should only please yourself, but you must first please yourself. When I say *everyone*, I'm only speaking of the most important people in your life. Your significant other and children, if you have any, are your priority. Also remember that if you care about every little thing someone says about the way you are, then you can look forward to spending the rest of your life trying to please everyone.

Rearview Mirror

The rearview is the mirror we use to see what's behind us. In a relationship, you should have no use for the rearview mirror. This mirror represents the past. If you have bugs smearing the windshield while looking in the rearview, you are sure to wreck your relationship. You should never bring up the past once you forgive someone. You should never bring past relationships' issues to your current relationship. You should never leave problems to resolve themselves, because they never do.

It took a whole lot of effort and praying, but above all, it took real change. We all know that change only occurs if you really want it. I say "real change," because more times then not, we say we are going to change but never do. I had to ask myself, "Why do I continue to do wrong?" If you have to ask yourself this, then maybe you shouldn't be doing whatever it is that you are doing. Make the right decision, do the right thing! Especially if you consider whatever it is that you are doing wrong, change your ways.

Finally, love God and then others!

Chapter 5
Four Stages of Misery

Before I get into the four stages of misery, I'd like to share a few things with you. This is very important. I'm quite sure you have at least heard of the show "Fear Factor." I'm not talking about being afraid to eat monkey brains or snails like contestants are on some reality television shows. I'm talking about being afraid to speak your mind when you have the chance. Men are guilty for just going with the flow with hopes that things will just fall into place. I could have saved my wife a lot of headaches if I would have just been real with her up front. It makes us feel like we are less manly if our significant others want something, and we really can't afford it. All we have to say is just that! Instead, we go with the flow and blame it all on them later. "You're the reason I have to work so much! You're the reason I can't do anything I want to do! You, you, you!" Sound familiar? If you can't be real with the woman you feel like you're breaking your neck to keep, then why are you with her? You have to have an honest open line of communication. This way you can avoid the *fear factor*. Normally how a man feels about the woman he's with has everything to do with the way she treats him. Questions we normally have for our wives include the following: Will you be supportive? How much are you willing to put up with? Are you willing to sacrifice? I can go on and on about what we expect from a woman, but the real question is, are you willing to give everything you are asking for? It's a two way street.

To my lady friends, hopefully you are reading this book with your man. Ladies please understand that a man needs to figure some things out on his own in order to feel like he's the king at least in his own home. Even if you bring home more money then he does, you have to allow him to be the man of the house. If you have what it takes to potentially make more money then he does, at no time should you make him feel like he can't do anything for you that you can't do for yourself. You will lose him. I promise you will push him away. He should want to be the provider, and you should let him. Even if he's making half of what you gross, allow him to be the man. This way you can cross out the resentment factor. If a man has a dream and you don't stand behind him, he will resent you, especially if he feels that it's the only way he'll be able to provide for you. Now, if he fails to reach his goal or goals, it's not your fault. But if you never support him, and he's forced to give it up for the mortgage, car note, and so on, he's going to shut down. He has financial anxiety. He feels like he has overextended himself. The heavier the responsibility load gets, the less real that reaching the dream becomes. He probably will not say it, but he will not be able to hide his resentment. I know every man chooses his own path. Sometimes the path he walks as a man was chosen as a child. Therefore the fear factor has kicked in, and the resentment factor is in play. Sometimes our best isn't good enough. If you are constantly in his ear about what he's not doing and what he needs to do, you will make him retreat to a relaxed atmosphere—in other words, you will make him retreat to another woman.

Going with the Flow

This section is also for my female readers: the last thing you want him to do is to feel like he's just going with the flow. This would be the first stage of misery. Now, for the men: how do you avoid the four stages of misery? First, you must be real with your wife up front. Never try to portray a person you think she wants you to be. Eventually the real you will come to the surface. Being that the first impression is by far the most important, you will be whoever she wants you to be in order to get that second date. You probably had no plans of going out as many times as you did. Who knew she was going to end up being the better half? She likes going to the opera, and you couldn't be real because of the way her face lit up, so you replied, "I love the opera!" This is how simple things get out of hand. So you've gone to the opera several times, and you've hated every moment. One year into the relationship, the brand new smell has gone away, and all of a sudden you decide you want to speak your mind. Problem number one: you've drawn the first red flag.

Routine

Stage number two is routine! After going with the flow for an insane period of time, it automatically becomes a routine. Believe me, I know! I married the woman I put on a front for. I was far from ready to be married, and it showed! I acted like I wanted what she wanted. She gave me the opportunity to be real with her before we went to the altar, but I just went with the flow. Six months into our marriage, things changed. I went from the honest hard working husband to the deceitful husband with inappropriate relationships on the side. Notice how I suddenly switched up the routine! This was always me. I had never closed that chapter of my life. I would only place a bookmark between the pages of that chapter. This way I could revisit whenever I felt the need to. Could all of this been avoided? Yes! All I had to do was continue to be myself from the beginning, and she would have been fine with us only being friends. But I wanted to have my cake and eat it, too. I wanted to change, but on my time. I was unfair to her, and I almost made a woman who loved me more then I loved myself hate me! I was okay with however and wherever she wanted to have the wedding, because I was feeling guilty. I went with the flow and changed up the routine! I had done so much wrong in our relationship, I felt the need to propose to her regardless of whether I was ready or not. *She's been here through it all. It's the right thing to do, right?*

Holding on to Time

Now that I've gone with the flow and established a routine, we've entered stage three, which is holding on to time. This is the worst thing anyone can do. I can't say it enough! It takes a continuous effort on both parts in order to have a successful relationship. With that being said, change is the only thing that is constant. Change will take place whether it's good or bad. My wife and I started dating at a very young age. She went from that little girl who accepts anything to that "I'm not having it!" grown woman. Things were perfect before we started growing apart. But it really wasn't that we grew apart; she grew up, and I didn't. This would most certainly be a conflict of interest. She had become a grown woman in love with a grown boy. She was misled. She thought that we had entered adulthood together. According to age, I was supposed to actually enter adulthood before her. The only thing that kept me from calling it quits was as simple as I needed her. I couldn't imagine waking up without her in front of me, and I really couldn't imagine her waking up with anyone else! Even when things got bad, we held on to those two young people in love. That beautiful college girl and that young, fly, hardheaded boy from the hood. Although she was my complete opposite, we fit like all the right pieces to a puzzle. At one point in time, we were all we had to hold on to. We made it through the storm with a lot of effort and prayer. Prayer cannot replace effort, and effort cannot replace prayer. You need to heavily rely on both. It was not easy for her. She always loved me, and she was always sure of that. I took her through a lot of unnecessary changes.

Pretending

Last but not least, pretending! Everything looks good from the outside looking in. On every occasion, you have to put on the "we're so happy" face! My wife will be the first to tell you that she's a pro at it. One thing she refuses to do no matter how bad she feels is let anyone see her hurt or angry. It was considerably easy for me to do, considering that I was always inflicting the pain. I was the one always telling the lies and constantly getting caught. It was as if I was addicted to the hunt. The sad part is she never gave me a reason. She didn't lack anything. She's as close to perfect as they come. Sure, she has a bit of attitude and says things that only God knows why. But overall, she's well-rounded and oh so beautiful inside and out. She's to be described as nothing less then an old soul in a young frame. They just don't make them like that anymore.

One of the hardest things I had to do was admit to cheating. My grandmother always said that what you do in the dark shall come to light. I had to tell her that I impregnated another woman. Not just any woman, but someone she attended school with. She was devastated! Once again, my boyish and irresponsible ways shadowed my manhood. This was yet another example of me just being a grown boy. I called her after I had received the results. How inconsiderate was I to tell her something of this magnitude over the phone instead of face-to-face? What a cowardly act on my part. Can you believe I actually considered myself a man? She was with her father at the time, but somehow she spoke to me as if nothing had happened. She bottled up that pain, swallowed her ego, and said, "Okay, babe, I'll talk to you later." This woman still married me with all my infidelities. Although this nearly tore us apart and I went to that altar feeling like I married out of guilt, from the outside looking in, we were the happiest couple on earth. How long can you pretend before you lose your sanity? How long can you pretend before your heart hardens and you lose face? You can only pretend so long before the truth eats away at your heart and settles on the surface where everyone can see.

Chapter 6
Romance Me

This chapter is set aside for both men and women. You have to be thoughtful year-round and not just during special occasions, such as Valentine's Day, anniversaries, etc. You shouldn't have to wait until Valentine's Day to tell her you love her. You don't have to wait until she wears something stunning and puts on makeup before you tell her how beautiful she is. You should not have to wait for Christmas in order to give her a "just because I appreciate you" gift. You shouldn't have to wait for another anniversary to come and go to realize that she's still there. Love her unconditionally! Majority of the women I've come across are blind to imperfections once they fall in love. I found myself criticizing my wife because she had put on weight. I made her feel uncomfortable in her own skin. She didn't like the fact that she had put on weight either. I went about things so wrong. I began to bring to her attention every time I thought she was overeating. She would have never done that to me. Everyone is different, especially when it comes to men's and women's bodies. It wasn't as easy for her to lose weight as it was for me. I had to realize that not everyone wants to run herself to death. I had failed my wife. I was far from being her support system. I used to think that she was lazy, and it seemed like every time we went for a run, she was making excuses. One morning she asked me if the room was spinning. I helped her get dressed and drove my wife to the emergency room. Shortly after the doctor returned, he told us that she had vertigo. This is when someone gets very dizzy; usually the person's equilibrium is off. It should not have taken this in order for me to back off. I felt so bad after that. I expressed to her how sorry I was for pushing so hard. I was thinking about myself. I was trying to get my wife back to a size six. I failed to realize that although she put on some weight, her love for me had never changed. I don't have a six-pack anymore, but she could care less. She still enjoys falling asleep to the rhythm of my heart. I've learned that she has changed on the outside, but her love for me has not. I love her! We've decided to get bikes and ride together. This way she can enjoy working out without getting dizzy. So you see, romancing each other is not just in the bedroom. Romance means understanding each other. It's communication! It's working together! If you don't remember anything else, note that romance is to love each other unconditionally.

Do unto others as you would have them to do unto you. It's in every Bible! Romance is not bias; it doesn't care about race, creed, or gender. As a man, when I say, "romance me," I'm asking to be treated like you want to be treated. I was told that actions speak louder than words! With that being said, how about you show me what you want? My wife feels as if I should be able to read signs. "Read the signs," she says! I asked my wife, "Why is it that you get so mad at me?" Her response was, "Because I tell you exactly what I want, and I also show you." She does have a point. Sometimes I get so tired I can't hear or see what she's saying. I'm big enough to admit that. Men, do your homework and study hard. If she begins to speak body language, and you are unable to interpret, you're in trouble. She then says, "You don't pay any attention to me!" If you're going through this with your significant other, just remember to be more attentive.

Attention, wives! Show your husbands how you want to be treated. Romance them! You want a bubble bath? So do they! You want a back rub? So do they! If it's okay for a woman to take over a once predominately male work industry and run for the presidency, then romancing her man shouldn't be a problem at all. Buy your husbands some flowers to show them how much you care. Remember this thing goes both ways. Hold tight, ladies; I know most of you also have to take care of the household on top of everything else. I'll now take this time to address the men.

Husbands, there are certain things that women can do that a man just cannot pull off. But anything a man can do to help out around the house, he should: cleaning, cooking, helping with homework, etc.

It's not about what's expected of men and women, it's about working together and doing whatever it takes to run the household. Note to self: if you have a superwoman, there's nothing wrong with preparing the meal and checking the kid's homework. Give her a break from the norm. To my wife, "hint": if you have a man who meets and goes beyond the call of duty, what's wrong with having his bath water ready upon his arrival from a hard day's work? My wife and I are both guilty of lacking in the romance department because we both have so much going on. We have two kids in the home, one outside the home, and twins on the way. They all require a lot of attention. I'm so thankful for my superwoman. We're the poor version of the Cosby Show. When we get stressed out, we have to keep the little things that count so much in mind. Whatever you have going on in your household, remember it's imperative that you find a way to keep the romance alive in your relationship. More importantly, it's not possible to be happy without God being first in your relationship. Happiness is nonexistent without romance in attendance.

Chapter 7
Foundation Built on Quicksand

Too much free time on a child's hands is dangerous. In a poem I wrote called "Our Rising Stars," I wrote, "babies having babies, undeveloped minds burdened with great responsibilities unable to finish high school" and "boys forced to become men fall victim to the system creating a frustrating atmosphere for themselves ... majority of the time dropping out of school. Having no education is like trying to complete a task without the right tools." We see this more times than not in sadistic subsidized housing communities. Once parents settle and become accustomed to this way of living, the majority of the time they fail to encourage their child or children to shoot for the stars. It's impossible to teach what you don't know, but if you want your child to succeed, you will find the answers to their questions. Either the child will welcome change and become adventurous, or the child will become uncomfortable with anything outside of what he is used to. He will acquire nothing more. This is when free time becomes a problem. The guys I grew up with had three options: they could envision becoming professional athletes, rappers, or hustlers. I tried as hard as I could to become one of the first two, but I chose to be like the majority—the hustler. Why? Because I didn't think I was smart enough to go to college. I felt uncomfortable around people I assumed I had nothing in common with. Instead of being the needle in the haystack, I chose to be part of the haystack.

If you call yourself a man, you have to take your place in the home. There are too many grown boys out there and not enough men. The ones who call themselves men are floating around planting seeds all over the place. They never come back to ensure that their child or children get what they need. I have all respect for every man who steps up to the plate—thank you! There are big brothers and after-school programs, which are all great, but we need fathers in the home. I've witnessed too many of my friends self-destruct because of a lack of parental guidance. The neighborhood does not make the hood the hood; the people in the neighborhood do. My grandmother laid a solid foundation. She tried her best to prepare me for the quicksand just outside the door. It was all around us. The quicksand was the shot house, the drug dealers, the drug addicts, the prostitutes, the thieves, the killers, and the alcoholics. An unconstructive environment doesn't have to always result in a dead end, but unconstructive thinking always does. In the hood, we are giving general knowledge of the streets and basic tools to survive. It's when we fail to attain an education that we drown in the world. Without direction, how can you find your way to success? Regardless of your context, you can succeed. The first step to success is to believe in yourself and make the best out of the resources available to you. My grandmother did everything to make sure I didn't sink. When she died; I failed to use the wings she left me to sore above it all.

Chapter 8
Living or Waiting to Die!

Life happens! Wouldn't you agree? I now realize that time is a privilege and should be handled with a sense of urgency. If you want to change your outcome, take a different approach. I can't say this enough! I've done some things in this flesh that even make me appalled at the sight of myself. If you live a deceitful and unjust life, the consequences will always be unpleasant. If you live an honest and righteous life, the outcome will be fruitful and fulfilling. I really want you to think about what I'm saying when I ask, "How do you want to be remembered on stage?" The world is your platform, and we all have a part to play. You could leave a lasting memory for an extraordinary and unforgettable act. You might not get the part you want, but it's all about how you play the part you are given. I've opened my eyes, and opportunity has never looked better. I've been trying to write my way out of poverty for at least ten years. I've taken breaks, but I've never stopped completely. I said I wanted to write for a living, and that's what I meant. I will write until somebody notices! I can't stop there. I have to make somebody notice! It's okay to put things in God's hands, but you have to play your part, as well. We are all either living or waiting to die! Many of us find ourselves having a dream at some point in our lives. We lose focus or let people discourage us along the way. What happens next is sad. We find ourselves just waiting to die. Passion is something you have to do, and that's what living is: doing what you love for a living. A job just to get by is slowly killing you. So are you living or waiting to die? I'm tired of being held prisoner to a lack of determination. I'm ready to start living!

This book is me taking my first breath. With Christ directing my life, along with my determination and faith, struggling is a piece of cake; struggling is nothing!

Struggle is the price we all have to pay in order to live. Here's a poem I wrote titled "Flour-N-Water." This title refers to the two main ingredients it takes to make bread. The bread I'm talking about is not the kind you eat, the way I use the word bread in this case represents money!

> I pulled out a spoon and bowl.
> I added a pinch of my heart and a dash of my soul.
>
> I'm determined to transform this flour and water into bread.
> Although my struggles have made me weak over time, I still have enough strength to hold up my head.
>
> I shower, eat, and sleep fully dressed with my eyes open, shoes on while in bed.
> I don't have time to lie down on sheets, but my ideas do. I live at my desk with a pen and a pad.
>
> Eyes are red, but still just flour and water—no bread.
> Terrified, to me failure is like a bully, and yes, I'm scared.
>
> What you need? I've got nicks, dimes, quarters, halves, Os, and pounds.
> That's not me now! I'm still grinding but with Christ, the word and advice, plus I have the time to share it with you now.
>
> How does that sound? If you didn't catch it, let me slow it down.
> Every day I'm hustling, every day I'm hustling!
>
> Don't get it misconstrued; don't assume I'm talking about baking soda mixed with powder to come back hard.

I'm talking about determination mixed with education to come back hard.

Either mix will get you a rock, but I'd rather pitch the one that's healing instead of the one that's killing.
There's more than one way to get money in your pocket from pitching a wonderful feeling.

So no matter what! I continue to hurdle over these obstacles, clearing disappointment and seeking success.
I have a few bellies to fill. I know I complain, but I still give God the praise because I know that I am truly blessed.

This battle is not mine alone; Lord knows this road to success might be complicated and long.
My hand gripped tightly around this pen, fingers doing reps, eyes push up on words, and I can feel my mind getting strong.

So my pen continues to lie between the sheets like the Isley Brothers.
Through sleet, snow, rain, and hail, I'm on block pitching my chronicles no matter the weather. I'm determined to get it together!

At times I get discouraged.
That's when I drop to my knees, and all of a sudden inspiration presents itself, and all of a sudden I'm encouraged.

I'm still working with nothing but this spoon and bowl.
So again and again, I add a pinch of my heart and a dash of my soul.

This flour and water is beginning to look like bread.
Eyes still red, no sleep, but it's just a matter of time now before I eat!

No matter what your passions are, you have to be willing to be successful or fail miserably trying.
If you don't make an attempt, believe it or not, from within you are slowly dying!

Chapter 9
Precious Minutes

If you really plan to succeed, you will! If you succeed at failure, it's because you didn't plan at all. I know it sounds silly, but doing nothing with your life is being successful at failure. In order to fail, all you have to do is absolutely nothing! Life is like the classroom. Everyone starts out with an A, but it's up to you to work even harder toward that A+ or decide not to care at all and do nothing to earn that F. As a man, you readjust several times with the hope of finally getting it right. When you find yourself displacing precious minutes, you must redirect your focus. You don't want to be on borrowed time, because time waits for no one. I should have published my first book ten years ago; that's how easy it is to displace precious minutes. You were getting high when you should have been in school. Maybe you were at a party when you should have been studying. I could go on and on about several different scenarios highlighting what we should've, could've, but didn't do. How critical is this? Displacing precious minutes can result in displacing life. I know you've heard "the right place at the right time"; how do you know if you have missed the right time while being careless with your precious minutes? Remember, every minute counts. Don't let your season past you by.

Do you really know the difference between a boy and a man? I was quick to lean on my mother every time discrepancies would rain; because I was old enough to be a man, my response was "I am man!" At least that's what I thought, but my actions didn't quite say the same. A man would never put his child in harm's way in order to chase money. I was taught that a man always keeps his priorities in order. I was told that all men should give and receive respect. First and foremost, they should always take care of their responsibilities. Patience is a virtue. A man weighs all his options and exploits all possibilities. I was hardheaded, and I didn't want to listen. My grandmother would always say "a hardhead makes a soft ass," and I almost missed the point. I was traveling through life entirely too fast. I am a man! At least that's what I thought. I was old enough to be labeled a man, but I still had a lot of childish ways. I was a grown boy taking everything for granted, too immature to acknowledge this phase. A man learns how to accept criticism; he leads by example. I thought I knew everything, but there was so much I did not know. 1 Corinthians 13:11 (KJV) "When I was a child, I spake as a child, I understood as a child, I thought as a child: but when I became a man, I put away childish things." I still had to grow! Everything that lives must die, and with that being said, you can never get those precious minutes back that you wasted. If you are taking life for granted, remember that no one is promised tomorrow.

Chapter 10
We're a Team

It's easy to get caught up in the pleasing everyone game. Just in case you didn't hear me the first time, I said, "Under no circumstances will you ever be able to please everyone!" In order to wrap your mind with peace, you must identify your priorities and take action. I drove myself crazy for years trying to make sure everyone was satisfied. In the process, I lost sight of what was really important in my life. Since the day I became a father, life has been challenging and very intricate. My wife has been here through it all. She has attended almost all of the child support and custody cases in the juvenile relations and domestic court. She was present during the criminal cases in the circuit court. She's been here through the anger management courses. She has given me peace of mind every time I had to turn myself in because of my extremely poor, irrational decisions. She has always been my support system. Can you believe that I was stupid enough to cheat on this angel? Yes, I've changed in many ways over the years, but she had to put up with many more years of womanizing before it all came to a complete halt. I'm not just speaking of sexual encounters. I'm talking about inappropriate relationships as a whole. I heard someone put it in perspective at my mother-in-law's wedding. The groom's brother said, "It was a tough catch, but it was an even tougher fisherman!" Thinking back to that time in my life, I really felt as if I was literally all over the place. It didn't have to be that way. I chose to bring three innocent children into the world out of wedlock. I chose to not be responsible. I chose this edition of trials and tribulations. I was scared to death when I found out about my first child. When I started dating my wife-to-be, I had to explain to her that I had two children by two different women. She was from a completely different background. I assumed I had a chance, but it was even harder to explain this to a mom with such high expectations for her daughter. I didn't understand then, but I fully understand now why she didn't want her daughter associating herself with a person of my caliber. I later found out I had a son as well, and she stayed with me after finding out about him. I still couldn't seem to find the balance. This almost destroyed us after we exchanged vows. I can't even begin to understand how she stayed here through it all. It had to be the presence of Christ. Although the kids seem to care only for their birth moms, my wife loves them like they were her own. Even when I let the kids' moms use me for the kids' sake, my wife understood. When I wanted to run away from fatherhood, my wife made me stay and fight. Whenever my faith would weaken and I went astray, my wife encouraged me to turn to the Lord and pray for direction. Even when the deceitful man she married proved ungrateful, she loved me. We learned a few things together. We learned that the children will try to play you against one another. Family will help you split apart if allowed. That's exactly why you have to remember, "We're a team!" You have to be reasonable, and you have to listen. You also have to communicate, be realistic, and, most importantly, support one another. You have to be willing to compromise, knowing things will not always go your way. You have to make rational decisions together. You have to be more then fair and always take your significant other's best interest at heart. You must see your significant other through your soul and not just through the set of eyes that comes with the flesh. In other words, you have to see eye to eye in the spiritual realm. The enemy is real, and there is nothing good about the flesh. The perfect relationship entails communicating and working things out. It entails making hard rational decisions together and attending family functions on both sides of the family. And it entails respecting each other, keeping the romance alive, and last but not least, loving hard and unconditionally. This is what being on the same team is all about. I've made a vow to see things from where my wife is standing. I want to show her how much I love her by being honest and as faithful as the vows we exchanged on November 5, 2005.

Chapter 11
Follow Through

How important is it to follow through? It's like taking the game-winning shot. Follow through and sink the basket, or don't follow through and watch the attempted shot hit the rim. In a relationship, you must follow through at all times. If you say you are going to complete a task around the house, do so. If your significant other asks you to do something, don't procrastinate. This is a good way to get into an argument. Simple things like this can be avoided. In life, you don't want to be known as the guy who never follows through. Believe me when I tell you, this is a hard title to shake. Especially on the job, the guy who never follows through also never gets promoted. Therefore your living standards never change.

In order to create good habits, you have to get rid of old bad habits. This is what I refer to as a "learning behavior." In order for something to become a habit, you have to include it in your daily routine. When I was chasing women, I was wasting precious minutes that I can never get back. I replaced those bad habits with writing and reading more. The combination of the two helped me to finish writing this book. You've been placed here on earth not just to succeed, but to empower so many others. Not just to learn, but to teach. It's imperative that you follow through in every aspect of your life. No more excuses! Life might beat you up from time to time, put a bump here and there, and it might even leave a scar. But just because you feel like life isn't being fair doesn't mean you need to use everything as an excuse to fail. You would rather make excuses than pick up the pieces and take that adverse situation as fuel to excel? We all have trials and tribulations. The first time around you might not clear every hurdle, but every challenge must be met in life. Anything worth having is worth working hard for, in all cases, which will require some kind of sacrifice. I'm guilty! We all have made excuses at some point in our lives. Keep God first, have faith, and believe in yourself. It takes no effort to fail, and it takes everything to succeed. Just take it one day at a time; set goals and then achieve them. Follow through!

Chapter 12
I See Her Now

The relationship had become routine; love decayed. This relationship could never reach new heights, and it was because of me. My entire life, I tore down women. I broke into their minds and walked away with their hearts, never looking back. From my first kiss in kindergarten to the loss of my virginity at age twelve, I've set out to get what I could get out of women. My misleading and deceitfulness were often disguised by charm. I was and am the reason for her nagging suspicion. I used to get upset because she would call my phone every five seconds. As so-called men, we often forget how our situations got so bad. More times than not, we made it that way! Why do we pursue what we already have at home? I'll tell you why: we think we love ourselves, even when we don't. It's like going to a buffet; you know you can't eat it all, but you try anyway. Men think; grown boys just do! Everyone is not as fortunate as I was. Attention all men! Please be very aware of the type of women you have. I would hate for you to trade in a Mercedes for a Ford—not that there's anything wrong with a Ford, but you get my point! Married for three, together for ten, and living under the same roof for almost four years, I had to bury the old me in order to see what was there all along, an angel! For years that front door would open and close. Sometimes she'd be leaving and sometimes coming home. I would always hear her voice, but that's it. It's now a blessing to be fortunate enough to glance in our wedding album while we share a couch. I can't believe she is still here. We often relive each moment page by page, getting lost in the moment as if we were there all over again. She was beautiful then, and she's even more beautiful now that I see her!

Chapter 13
Several Deaths, One Burial

Life is sort of like a dinner plate. Sometimes we put things on it, assuming we'll like the way they taste based on how they look. I look back on the type of life I've led and often ask myself, why did I put that on my plate? I'm quite sure you've heard the phrase, "Everything that looks good isn't good for you." Could it be that our eyes are bigger than our stomachs? My grandmother used to say that every time we'd put too much on our plates. That's how I know I never became a man; I just got older. All the way up to age twenty-nine, I had an appetite for destruction. The world had become my buffet, and I attempted to eat as much as possible. I had a sweet tooth, and sin was the dessert that fulfilled my cravings. I didn't pick the nutritious healthy entrée because it was good for me. There's a significant difference between life and a plate of food: if you don't like something you put on your plate, you can just put it back. But if you chose to eat from the world's buffet, once you put a bad decision on your plate, you can't just put it back. You have to make real change in your life in order to enjoy the fruits of life.

The Lord said to do unto others as you would have them do unto you. The plate you fix for someone else might be the meal that you have to eat. Several deaths, one burial! What does this mean? Born into sin, we have to deny the flesh every single day. Men are expected to fall because of the hand of a woman. It's been that way since the beginning of time. Men are weak in the flesh; therefore we die every single time we ask for forgiveness and move on. The problem with this is that too many times we revisit that chapter in our lives and fall short of the glory of God. Instead of closing the chapter, we place a bookmark there so we can pick up where we left off. Several deaths, one burial! In order to stop dying over and over again from your infidelities, you have to bury that past version of yourself. Ask God into your life and start living. I attended a service where the pastor shook up the sanctuary. He spoke from the Old Testament, the book of Job. If you don' know the story, Job was a righteous man who the Lord allowed Satan to test. He had what the pastor called "fixed faith in the Lord." Faith is the substance of things hoped for and the evidence of things not seen. Job was around before Christ walked the earth; therefore he had to have faith just like each man today. The only proof he had was the same proof we have today. Unlike us, Job was God-fearing and faithful, and he still had trials and tribulations. The pastor said, "You can't worry about everything and everyone around you," meaning that you have to first worry about your own salvation. Just like today, family and friends tried to deter him from his faith in the Lord. He trusted in God, and he ended up on top. He lost his children, his livestock, and his health, but the one thing he didn't lose was his faith. He came out of all this with three times as much. Trust in the Lord, and he shall over fill your cup with more blessings than you have room to receive. He had fixed faith! The pastor also said that it's a fixed fight. If you know anything about boxing, the boxer the fight is fixed for always wins, even when the fighter appears to be fighting a losing battle. Put the Lord in your corner, and I guarantee if you have fixed faith, regardless of how bad things seem, the results are always the same: in your favor! A God-fearing man is a found man, and a man who depends on his own judgment is forever lost.

Chapter 14
Genetics or Excuses

If you have a dad, uncle, older brother, grandfather, etc., I'm sure you've heard this before: "Boy, it's in your blood!" Every time my father and I go out to shoot a few racks of pool, we speak on the topic of "why most men want to do right." From his perspective, it's more like why men in our family can't do right. The answer is always the same: "it's in our blood." That's when the million-dollar question comes up: is it genetics or excuses? Prior to the burial of the old me, I used this line as an excuse all of the time. My father's tendencies even went back as far as his father and my great-grandfather. All my uncles are the exact same way. It appears that the apple does not fall far from the tree.

It took me all of this time to realize that I had always had a choice. Being dishonest is not in my blood or in my heart. Being that way was only in my mind. I choose differently now. Neither my father nor my uncles have had a successful and honest relationship. How can you teach what you've never done? Even before I got married, I entertained bad advice. I wasn't smart enough to pay attention to details. If every guy who had a bad experience in his marriage gave me bad advice, what would I really have to look forward to? I would wonder whether there really is anything good about being married. Some of the same men who spoke so badly about their marriages are still married to the women who are supposedly making them so miserable. Does that sound right to you? Instead of going straight home from work, they would rather hang around their drinking buddies. I should have removed myself from those conversations as soon as they began to take the negative approach. I allowed myself to get caught up in something that would end up affecting me later. It's like me trying to tell you how to make a million bucks, yet I'm poor. That's what we do every time we take advice from someone who has yet to figure out the course himself. In other words, these men should ask, "How can I teach you something I do not know?"

Sometimes the best lessons in life are through other people's examples. I don't care what your father, grandfather, uncles, or your big brother did. You are still an individual! They can't go to heaven or hell for you. You have to make that decision for yourself. You must have a craving to do right and a strong will to stay the course. The ways of the world aren't in your blood, nor are they in your heart. The process begins with your mind as a child, and it's not easy to undo whatever it is that you have been taught to do as a child. But once you're old enough to understand right and wrong, you must seek knowledge and understanding. Since knowledge begins with the fear of the Lord, how can a man who does not keep God's commandments teach you the right things? Attention, all men! It's imperative that you teach your children about God, but more importantly, show them how to walk in this world by way of example. Telling them one thing and doing another only confuses them. I've heard parents tell their children, "Do as I say, not as I do!" More than likely, their parents told them the same thing. By continuing to pass on bad information from generation to generation, we will keep ourselves and our children in bondage.

PART 2

My Story

Chapter 15
Early Childhood Development

How did I get here? I asked myself this over and over again! *How did my life play out this way?* It was like my life had once again been altered overnight. In jail, I thought to myself, *Here I am, locked up at the age of twenty-one with serious charges over my head.* It wasn't always that way. I was born Johnta Devon Knight on July 20, 1978 in Portsmouth, Virginia. The Lord placed me in the hands of a loving family. I was raised in a diminutive community by the name of Huntersville, located in Northern Suffolk, Virginia. Can you say ghetto? Even though my neighborhood would be considered the slums to corporate America, to me it was home sweet home. We didn't have time to think about how poor we were growing up. My grandmother drilled a few essential statements into our heads. "You are blessed!" "There are a lot of people less fortunate than you, and things could be a lot worse." She would always say, "God is good!" I was around the age of thirteen when I responded to that statement for the first time. I replied, "If God is so good, why does he allow us to live in these run-down houses? Why is it that more than half of the people in this neighborhood are without bathrooms or running water?" She replied, "Boy! God is good, and don't you ever forget that!"

As a kid I was too embarrassed to invite any of my classmates over. I use to get off the bus in front of a decent house in a nearby neighborhood by the name of College Square. I didn't want anyone laughing at my house. Above all, I hated those kerosene heaters! Everything that I wore smelled like kerosene. I stood at the bus stop just outside my home at least a half hour earlier with the hope that my clothes would air out before I attended school. Maybe I would smell like gas or maybe not. I can't necessarily say that everything was appalling in my neighborhood. We did have the neighborhood chicken shack, which was my aunt Lovie's pad. Have you seen *The Color Purple?* Her shack was the modern day joop joint, only fifteen paces behind her house. Then there was the corner store. There was never a dull moment in that sector of the hood. If you wanted to learn how to hustle, fight, shoot dice, or steal, all you had to do was post up just outside Eddie Ward's corner store. This was the heart of the hood. This is where tainted blood rushed through the veins of those arctic streets. Directly across the boulevard was the neighborhood shot house. If you're not familiar with the term "shot house," it's where they serve the cheapest liquor in the world. According to the hood alcoholic's rave reports, it served its purpose. It was that corner where everything violent occurred and everything else that was illegal took place. We also had a dance hall next to the corner store known as "the hall." Although our neighborhood was small, people feared it because of its rough appearance. Huntersville was one-way in and one-way out. Certainly if you where not from around there, or you didn't know anyone, it was not in your best interest to press your luck by passing through. We fought each other on a daily basis, so imagine what happened to uninvited guess. Bounded by poverty, almost everyone in my neighborhood was insolvent; all but a few drug dealers were extremely broke. At this time, they didn't know how to change their situations.

It's hard to believe in the late eighties that some people still didn't have a bathroom or running water. The only thing available to most people at this time was outhouses and pumps. If you're not familiar with the term, an outhouse is few pieces of ply board, so you could have some privacy, and a bucket with a toilet seat on top of it. If you really wanted to be classy, you would dig a hole about 3 feet deep, but not too wide. You wanted the bucket to be larger then the hole. This way the urine and everything else would go directly into the ground. Seasons change, and life in the winter wasn't all that great. You had two options in the winter. You could freeze your tail off literally while on the bucket, or keep the bucket in the house. Unfortunately, you would have to put up with a horrendous odor throughout your home. Trust me when I say we literally put up with a lot of crap! I guess you could say we had the first portable potties. What is a pump? A pump was a means of survival used by people who could not afford running water. This was some of the best tasting water, especially if you were really thirsty. After it would rain, we gathered a few cups and bottles. Then we would acquire some water from the nearest ditch. This was so we could get the pump started. To some, that's hard living, but to us, that was everyday life.

There was nothing optimistic outside of the windows through which we viewed the world. There were no community centers or any big brother programs. The only thing that was remotely positive was the church. My grandmother kept me in church as much as possible. I'm talking about choir rehearsals, church revivals, Bible study, weddings, Sunday school, morning service, and funerals. It didn't matter what the affair was. She was fine with it as long as it took place in church. Even with all of the church events I had to take part in, for some reason trouble still found time for me. I must admit I had a lot of help picking up bad habits along the way. My oldest and only brother on my father's side was considered a hardhead or, shall I say, a thug. I wanted to be just like him. He still doesn't know that. My whole way of thinking switched up once my brother was incarcerated for gunning a man down. He was sentenced to twenty-six years for the crime. Lucky for him, in 1991 you only had to do 50 percent of your time. He completed twelve years with the help of some good behavior. He went into the penitentiary at the age of eighteen and was not released until the age of thirty-one. The story he gave me was probably the same story I gave the judge when I was on trial, my version of the truth. He allowed himself to become another statistic like so many others before him. I'm not trying to validate anything using race or context. I will not be making an attempt to shift blame by leaning on the typical "poor black boy from the ghetto" excuse as a defense. But in my brother's defense, he grabbed the bull by the horns. He was raised in a pessimistic environment without MapQuest. Let's just say this jungle didn't come with directions. It was sink or swim! He chose to swim straight to the bottom. To a certain extent, I do blame our father for not spending any time with my brother. He allowed the streets to raise his son and mold his mind, and he failed to protect his son from the very corners that whispered sweet nothings into his ears. Although my father played a modest part in my life until I was ten, a lot of that quality time was spent sitting on the armrest in his car. I was part of the "kiss the sky" crew. I never willingly smoked anything, but being in the presence of him and his friends would have me buzzing from secondhand smoke. My father most definitely gave in to temptations. Poppa was a rolling stone indeed! He and his partners enjoyed their joints and thunderbirds. There I was, sitting on the armrest in a car full of smoke. I must say, he was quite the toaster. I know what you're thinking: "What a role model!" My father was a womanizer! Prioritizing was not one of his strengths. Discrepancies began to rain after he lost his job at the shipyard, which is where I'm currently employed. The inevitable happened. He began testing positive for drugs, and shortly after, he forgot all about us. By the time I was eleven years old, my brother had already started doing his time in prison. My father was nowhere to be found. At this point, only God and the dope man could lay a hand on him. My aunt was also a point of contact, and he would send her "I'm still alive" messages. He would only contact her every now and then. After a while, I couldn't care less whether he was alive or not.

Evangeline Knight, my mother, was always there for me. She did the best she could by herself. My sister Amanda was also like a mother to me. She was extremely close in age to our mother. My mother gave birth to Amanda at the age of twelve. Unbelievable! My sister Veronica and I also had a very close relationship. My relationship with my baby sister, Arshay, is a little different. We were just so far apart in age. I still love her just the same. My mother had two kids by the age of fifteen, and three by the age of twenty-one. Luckily, my grandmother was there to take most of the responsibility off of her. She allowed my mother to have a childhood in spite of her situation. My grandmother raised all of us until my mother was ready to step up. Dorothy Mae meant everything to us. She was the very definition of life. She was my big momma! If anyone had a problem, she always had the solution. She would comfort you in any situation. From finances to just good old moral support, she was always there. You could always depend on my Dorothy Mae! Although I grew up in a sadistic setting, she was the umbrella that protected me whenever problems would downpour. She certainly was the sunshine that pushed the clouds away. She touched a lot of people's lives while she was here on earth. She gave birth to a total of five children. Our family would extend beyond imaginable. She ended up with a total of twenty-three grandchildren. Unfortunately, not all of her grandchildren were able to meet her before she died. For the ones who were, she made every single one of us feel as if we were the special grandchild. She had a way of showing you how much she loved you. She found the time to build a relationship with each and every one of us. Anyone fortunate enough to have crossed her path could vouch for her beautiful spirit. I remember when my cousins and I would get into an argument. We would throw whatever our grandmother did for us in one another's face. That's when we found out that she was not treating either of us any better than the other. That's when we found out that we all were her favorite. Dorothy Mae Borrow was an angel in disguise. Of course, she was unknown to those who never met her, but those who knew her will never forget her. I miss her so much! It's because of the way she raised me that I eventually straightened out somewhat. I'll never forget what she told me when I was about thirteen years old. "When I leave this earth, if you ever go out there in those streets, the Lord will bring you back willingly or on your knees!" I had been kicked out of school for shoplifting while on a fieldtrip to Busch Gardens. Backpedaling a few years prior to this incident, I attended an event called Scared Straight. I drew a knife on another kid in the presence of an officer. I was under the influence of a group instead of being an individual soaring above the influence. My grandmother always said, "You could never make right from wrong." She always had a quote, but this statement stuck with me, "You will always have a relationship with Christ; if you should ever go astray, he will bring you back." At the time, those words didn't mean anything to me, but I will go on to explain how that statement made me reevaluate myself.

Chapter 16
Glory Days

After being kicked out of school at the end of my eighth grade year, I reexamined myself. I made up my mind! I would at least finish high school. What's so hard about showing up and doing just enough to get by? Who cares if I graduate with a 3.0 or 2.0 as long as I graduate, right? Well, if you decide to be average, you will become average. It is a horrible routine. You get used to finishing last, and that's okay, right? Who knew that the way I carried myself in high school would be the way I carried myself in the real world? Are you satisfied with the way you went about or are going about preparing yourself for the real world? Are you just another average person, or are you making preparations to become just that? How can you possibly be shooting for the stars if you plan to never leave the ground?

I attended Nansemond River High School located in Suffolk, Virginia. I had no responsibilities, and I was involved in three different sports. I was considered an athlete student instead of a student athlete. What's the difference? A student athlete puts his or her academics first. I was quite the contender in track and field. Some of the events in which I would compete were the 100 meters, 110-meter hurdles, and the 400-meter relay. Although I was only weighing in at 155 pounds soaking wet, I played every sport like a giant. My football coach told me that it wasn't the size of the dog in the fight; it was the size of the fight in the dog. He considered me a small guy with a big heart. Every week I was in the *Suffolk News Harold*, a local paper. We also had a small pamphlet that gave a description of each player. I never made it past high school. I was good enough, but my grades weren't. Who cares about the once talented player with an extremely low grade point average? I started on both sides of the football. At the time, we were only AA, but we had a lot of talent on the field. We made a lot of noise on Friday nights. I would run out on that field feeling superior! I was exactly where I needed to be; I couldn't think of anywhere else in the world I would have rather been at the time. I also played basketball. I made the team because of my tenacious defense. I used to annoy players so badly that they literally wanted to fight me. What can I say? It was part of my character anyway.

I was also known for dating a girl with the same name as I. I was doing the same thing then as I would continue to do many years out of high school. I was sleeping with every girl who was a jock groupie or who just had a thing for me. My chain of bad habits began way before my adulthood; I just didn't notice. Could this have been because of the generation curse, or genetics? I also had my eye on a freshman that would later become my wife. She had big glasses, a very small frame, and she also whore braces. She was a cheerleader and heavily involved in every school club. A woman with beauty and brains! She was exceedingly intelligent. She was too young for me, so I used to just flirt with her. I told her that I would come back for her once she was older. She would smile, but she wasn't exactly your typical young female without any sense. I was coming to the tail end of my senior year, and I wished Kellen the best. I told her that I'd catch up with her in the real world.

There I was thinking to myself, *what I'm I going to do now?* I never planned to do anything outside of sports. I assumed that I would turn pro in some sport and that life would be peaches and cream. It never occurred to me that a million other kids had the same dream. I had a rude awakening! Reality set in, and I stopped playing sports. My coach didn't have anything to do with me after I started something I couldn't finish. As you can see, the pattern started early on in my life. I had no idea that those decisions I made in high school would define me. Everyone assumed I stopped playing to focus on my grades, but I actually wasn't doing anything in school. I could fool everyone but myself and God. I had a 1.9 grade point average. I stopped playing because I wasn't eligible. This is what usually happens when parents assume they know what's going on. My mother had not seen any of my report cards since I was in the seventh grade. Poppa was still nowhere to be found at this point. I'd been living so many lies for so long that I had become a complete stranger to that person in the mirror. The lies always started out small. They eventually evolved into something beyond my control. Neither my mother nor my father graduated from high school. Even if my father had been around, he probably would not have been involved much. He spent most of his time running the streets. I could have been a gymnast, and yes, maybe I could have been good enough to compete in the Olympics. Maybe I could have dribbled my way out of the hood. I could have just as easily attended a four-year college and used the brain the good Lord gave me. But we all know that those "maybes, could'ves, and should'ves" have never been and will never be good enough. That's a fact! I didn't graduate with honors or with an athletic scholarship. Instead I graduated without a clue of what I was going to do with the rest of my life. It was at that moment I was unsure of myself for the first time. It was all over for Mr. Popular. Who really remembers that guy? I wasn't as confident as I was on Friday nights when I wore that uniform. I had already begun to miss the saccharine taste of victory and the crowd chanting vigorously while the band would play. I was about to enter the real world with no plan. My grandmother was no longer there to pick up the slack for me, but my mother was still there. She did all she could for me. She loves me as much as a mother could love her child. I remember my name being mentioned for the very last time in that stadium. After I received my diploma, I took one last glance at the football field inside Arrowhead Stadium. I then looked to the heavens. I vividly remember a scene so calm with blue skies. At that very moment, I could feel my grandmother's presence. On that day, she was so proud to see me walk, but I knew she was disappointed in me at the same time. Just like that, the glory days for me had come to an end. This was the ending to the beginning of the rest of my life.

Chapter 17
Making Money Hand Over Fist

I had no intention of playing college football or basketball. My focus had been redirected to the streets. The older I got, the less real becoming the next Michel Jordan had become. He was no longer my role model. I started looking up to the select few cats who became hood rich. The chances of meeting Jordan or dribbling my way out of the hood were slim to none. I started settling, just as I did for that C or D on my report card. I began to lean more toward the neighborhood rock stars. What's the irony of it all? My reach was too short to get a grip on reality.

My cousin Yhamma had been getting paper since the late eighties. I remember when he had a money-green Impala with the flakes in the paint. He also had some rims on his whip and piped butter leather seats. His partner had a banana ninety-eight with a burgundy ragtop. He also had burgundy pin stripes, and the interior was crushed velvet. They were pimping rides long before Xzibit. They were getting more money back in the day than most hustlers had seen in their entire career. They stuck out like needles in a haystack. Once you reach this level, there is no turning back. They were the only ones in the neighborhood at that time with fly rides and gold jewelry. They also rocked diamond-studded earrings. They where young, fresh, and flashy! I wanted to be just like them. If I asked Yhamma for a dollar, he would pull out a couple of bankrolls with rubber bands wrapped around his dough. This made him feel superior to the next. He would do all of this just to give me a five-dollar bill. You probably think that they should not have been keeping that much money on them. With an attitude and a few guns, who's going to run up on you? My cousin was like a conductor with two guns that made beautiful music. He was another classic example of a person lacking education. How much of a return shall you receive on money sitting in a few mattresses and shoeboxes? Absolutely nothing! What good is a cluster of money if your name and status don't match? My cousin's lack of education proved to cause his inevitable demise.

My grandmother on my father's side passed away shortly after my cousin was incarcerated. I can't recall spending a lot of time with my father's parents. I do recall my grandfather John's demeanor being considerably rough around the edges. According to my father, his parents meet in the penitentiary. I see why he's so tough! I can remember everything as if it happened yesterday. My aunt had to pay the state in order for my cousin to attend the funeral. He arrived in shackles and chains, but even at that moment, all I could see was the money and cars. I still wanted to be young, fresh, and flashy. He came home somewhere around 1996. I remember this because a partner I grew up with got arrested. At the time, my boy who got arrested was three weeks away from graduation. People make mistakes, but guns don't. The end result was that someone took a bullet to the face. Just like that, his life had also been altered overnight. Remember what I said about being cautious of the decisions you make? Very important! Yhamma tried staying out of trouble. But when you have a hustler's mentality, you implement whatever it takes to make your life bearable. Believe me when I tell you that ten times out of ten you will go with what you know. You guessed it, a couple of years later, he fell right back into the trap. It almost never fails. You know what they say; "once a part of the system, always a part of the system!" It's hard to go from beans and franks to steak and then back to beans again.

When I was about eighteen and ready to grind, I approached him with the mentality of a hustler, but I was as green as the product I was trying to distribute. From athletics to pharmaceuticals—who knew? My cousin gave me my first ounce for free. That's fifteen ounces short of a pound, which is a joke. He started me out with one at a time. I can't say that he gave me consignment, because he didn't want any money back. If you don't understand the term *consignment*, it's when someone fronts you something and they expect something back. On the streets, paying this kind of loan back isn't optional. Depending on whom you're dealing with, the consequences could be quite severe. Cats on the grind are known to be worrisome. After going back to see him the fourth time, he told me that he couldn't look out for me anymore. He told me straight up, "You don't know how to hustle." He said I should have come back to him and purchased more than he gave me. What did he expect? This was fast money. I had to get used to it, and so what if I tricked a little bit? *Tricking* means to blow everything on nothing. He then went on to say that if I was really serious about getting ahead in this game, I needed to buckle down and stick to the script! I was young and dumb, and all I was interested in was women, shoes, and clothes. Instead of flipping my money, I was tricking my money. The drug game was designed to double, triple, or maybe even quadruple your paper. What's the point in hustling backwards? If every time you re-up, you copped the same weight, there's no sense in doing it. I had to understand that I was going about it the wrong way. Selling drugs wasn't for everybody. People from the outside looking in only saw the glamorous life. But people knee deep in the game, the ones who take all the risk, could care less about the repercussions.

Have you ever heard the term "guns don't kill people; the streets kill people!" Well the streets aren't deceitful, just the people in the streets are. My cousin was trying to tell me not to trust anyone in this line of work. He said that either they're trying to make money or take money! I was running with a live wire, and all I had to do was find a decent connection. I wish it were that simple. I knew a few people who were doing their thing, but I was so new to the game. I didn't think that any of them would have anything to do with me. I approached a couple of them, and I told them all the same story. "I can put you on to a nice low-key spot. There's a lot of money to be made." Some of them took me for a joke. The ones who were interested gave me the third degree. I was young, wild, hungry, and broke. I was also blessed with the gift of gab. I convinced this connect to hit me with consignment. He fronted me my first pound, and I thought I was the man! I had never seen that much weed at one time in my life. I had mixed feelings about it at first. I talked a good game, but I didn't have the clientele. I had been selling nicks and dimes, which was considered petty weight. I must say, that low-key spot was a gold mine. It started slow, but it picked up in no time. A Spanish female I was dating at this time use to help me bag up, and she kept the product on her. How real is that? She helped me turn my money over a few times. We decided to mix business with pleasure, and that's when our relationship folded. That beautiful run came to an end. Once again, I let my small head make a decision without consulting my big head. There are rules to this game.

I quickly got addicted to making money hand over fist. All I had to do was hand someone a product and receive some cash. How easy is that? Open hand over closed fist! It's a simple and quick transaction. After getting pimped for so long, I finally learned how to pimp the game. I started saving every penny. I stopped taking fronts, and I started getting a much better return. I didn't have someone calling me every five seconds asking me for his money. I could take my time and stretch it as much as I wanted to. If I spent seven hundred on a pound, I was trying to make at least sixteen hundred back. I was in no rush, and so I broke every pound down to nicks, dimes, quarters, and halves. I wanted every dollar possible. I took some of my re-up money and dabbled into some other avenues. I started with an eighth of hard white. That's powder cocaine mixed with baking soda to create what you may know as crack. I flipped that for a minute. But I never purchased more then a half. About a year into the game, I noticed that I was running in place. I was making money, but I wasn't making any real money. At this time, I still couldn't find a decent connection, so I slowed down. Indictments were being handed out like they were going out of style. College Square was extremely hot! On fire, baby! There were a few guys whom I grew up with who had become strung out. One of the ten crack commandments states, "Never get high off your on supply." Except these cats were handling bundles—heroin. They had started breaking into any and everybody's homes to support their habits. They had that monkey on their backs, and they couldn't shake it. They went from being distributors to users. A couple of guys used to OD on heroin like they could care less whether they lived or died. They had been trying to get money just like I was, and the majority of them had been in the game a lot longer then I had.

Most of these guys' parents where alcoholics and users. The streets raised most of them. Could you imagine raising yourself? Could you imagine your mother having sex with your peers to support her habit? When I was a freshman in high school, I used to watch these guys pile up on the same corner. They all stumbled in pursuit of the same hood dream. You snooze, you loose! There was never enough money to go around. Not exactly the winter games, but it was their Olympics. They were considered track stars. They would run after money all day. They were known as acrobats flipping product from sunup to sunset. The difference in the reward was that they didn't play for medals; they played for keeps. Life as a dealer isn't all that great. It's not as glamorous as it might appear from the outside. Fast money, sex, drugs, and deception are one hell of a combination. Money hand over fist; all it took was one transaction, and I was hooked! After being harassed by the cops, having to throw away work, and almost getting caught several times, my conscience started to kick in. I decided to slow down and enjoy the view. I gave up making money hand over fist for school and an honest paycheck. At least I thought I was getting my life together. To quote one of my poems,

> I'm from the bottom, where we only see successful people on TV. I'm from a place where 99.9 percent out of a hundred possesses the blueprint for failure. Paraphernalia runs first leg, and to bring it home we depend on arm and hammer. It's just like the summer Olympics: nothing but gymnasts on the block powdering their hands and flipping until they land up in the slammer. No bank account, just the bamma, knots in sox. No Bank of America, Wachovia, or Sun Trust. The only bank sons trust is a Timberland or a Nike Air box. The streets took the place of our fathers, and we listened to them and not our mothers! All of the resources we used to get to the top landed us right back at the bottom. It's all good! Don't worry about us; we'll survive—down here at the bottom!

Chapter 18
The Beginning of Accepting Failure

I barely graduated; that's right, barely! That prominent future and all those dreams of becoming a professional athlete had vanished. The kid that everyone expected to make it had become a disgrace to his grandmother. All she wanted is for me to attend college and excel. That's all she asked of me before she passed away. I felt like I let everyone who supported me down, as well as myself. A lot of people from my neighborhood attended my games on Friday nights. My mother could not be in attendance because she worked nights. Shortly after graduation, I attended ITT Technical Institute. My mother tried to keep me away from the ways of the world, but her attempt was only through words, not by example. What I thought was just a phase had become a routine. I didn't finish ITT, either.

Approximately one year out of high school, I had the most disturbing phone call of my life. A young lady I hooked up with once or twice had been trying to reach me. I had already braced myself for the worst. Now the question at hand was, "What's the appalling news?" The phone call went something like this. I called and asked to speak to her.

She answered, "Hello?"

"This is Johnta," I replied.

She said, "What's up?" I could tell she was hesitant. She appeared to be frantic about something. "Are you sitting down?" she asked.

At this point, I was extremely nervous. I had slept with so many females at this point in my life without protection; I assumed she was going to tell me that she had AIDS. My heart was pounding! I went on to ask, "What's wrong?" I had become very impatient. "Just say it!"

She then replied, "I'm holding your daughter as we speak."

I screamed out overwhelmingly, "What!" I began to have mixed emotions before she could get it all out. I must admit, I was perplexed and petrified. My heart was racing and palms sweating profusely. I replied, "What do you mean you're holding my child?"

"I was not planning on telling you; it was my mother's idea," she said. I told her that I would be over with my sister. That was the last thing I said before we hung up phone. Confused now more then ever, I told my sister Amanda what was going on. My cousins of course thought that this was hilarious. We were young at the time, so they didn't know any better. My sister flipped out! Even though my possible baby's mother only stayed a few miles away, this had to be one of the longest rides I've ever taken. Momma's baby; poppa's maybe! I had butterflies in my stomach. Once we arrived, the butterflies turned into an anxiety attack. A few moments later, there I was, standing outside her door, thinking to myself, *It's too late to run now ... here goes nothing.* The door swung open, and there she was, holding a baby. I can't even explain how I was feeling inside. I had been having so much unprotected sex prior to this situation, but no one else had turned up pregnant. Only a young, dumb, uneducated kid would think along those lines.

I eventually got around to taking a blood test. At the age of nineteen, who's ready for a responsibility like that? After the results came back, I was in trouble. The deadbeat dad campaign was going strong thanks to guys like my father! All of a sudden, every man in America was the villain, and every single mom was the victim. I'm not saying that some guys didn't deserve it, but some just got caught in the cross fire. Five minutes after the results came back, I lost my virginity to the child support system. This was just the beginning of my bad luck streak. I received even more disturbing news. Another woman went on to tell me that she was pregnant. She said, "Don't even think about asking me to get an abortion."

There I was, just turning twenty years old, and I had no clue of how I was going to take care of these children. I had no idea of what I was going to do with the rest of my life. I began to hustle harder than ever. I panicked! I could barely take care of myself. Now I had one child and another on the way, and by two different women. I was in and out of work. I felt like college really wasn't for me. Just like one of the typical hood dreams, all I had was my music. We all know that breaking into the industry is like trying to win the lottery. I graduated in 1997, but I started writing poetry in 1994. By 1996, I went from writing poetry to reciting lyrics. At first, I didn't take myself seriously. After I really started to pursue it in 1998, I took some product on consignment. This was one of my many contradictions; I revisited a place to which I said I would never go back. I would then take the money I made and invest it in myself. Then I would book studio time and work on some material. I would take the rest of the money and re-up (buy more product) in order to keep making money. I was chasing the dream while taking care of my reality. I still had to take care of myself and two children. I must admit, child support was killing me! But that didn't slow me down. I started having sex with even more women. I began to notice that I was becoming my father. I became the one person whom I resented at the time. I started taking life for granted as if I was incoherent at all times. I was living life dangerously. What's more dangerous than a black man without a plan in America?

It seems the older I was getting, the less responsible I was becoming. I was only using condoms when I had them, when I should not have been fornicating in the first place. What's wrong with that picture? You should never have unprotected sex under any circumstances. Pregnancy should be the least of your problems with all the diseases out there. Some choices that we make in life can only be made once. There's no turning back! I would help women with their poor decision to deal with me for many years. I had become addicted to fast money and allergic to being broke. I started recording in several different studios and attending workshops. After showing people how hungry I was, I didn't have to spend my bill money to support my dream anymore. The first person who believed in my project besides me was my cousin Gary. I admire that guy a lot. He's considered a pioneer by hood standards. He's what we would call an "all-around hustler." You can't get a business loan from the bank to become a rap star. That's where my cousin came into the picture. He had his own barbershop, among many other successful businesses. He supported me to the fullest. Yes, he was a businessman, but he genuinely wanted to see me do well. I had posters and CDs all over the shop. There it was, 1998, and I was trying to break into the industry. But having a successful music career requires patience, money, and a lot of time. Although he couldn't put anymore money into my project, I really appreciated everything that he had done. This was just the boost of confidence I needed to excel. I kept pursuing music.

While all of this was going on, I happened to bump into an old friend. I was taking a break from the streets and playing ball with one of my younger cousins, and out of nowhere, she appeared. A healthy young lady jumped onto my back. There she was, Kellen Fladger. I couldn't believe my eyes, she was so beautiful! She looked so different from the last time I had seen her. She wasn't wearing glasses or braces, and she had picked up some weight. She was about a hundred pounds the last time I had seen her. I was astounded, and so we began to converse. She was so different from the type of women I was dealing with. I wasn't just infatuated with her outer appearance; it had a lot to do with how well she spoke. I was used to the hood rats. She was so young, yet so classy. We had a diminutive crush that had the potential to grow into something special. Kellen was the typical goodie girl. You know the old saying, "Good girls love bad boys." Nevertheless, I wasn't sure if I wanted to get involved just yet. I had too much on my plate already. Things didn't quite work out the way I had planned. I had only planned to see her a few times. I ended up meeting her stepmom first. Although she had a few questions for me, she was pretty cool. Her first question was a typical one. "What's your line of work?" Then she followed that questioned with, "Are you currently in school?" Last but not least, "What are your plans?" I played it cool because I really didn't have any. Then I met her father. I was expecting Conan the Barbarian, but he ended up being laid back. It was her mother who was the aggressive one. I thought to myself, *I made it past the father; the mom should be a piece of cake.* Boy, was I wrong! Her mother was hell on wheels! She had zero tolerance for nonsense! The first time I shook her hand, I was looking for her balls. Love you, Mom, but it's the truth. She replied, "You call that a handshake?" Lesson number one: always shake hands with a nice, firm grip. I received my second strike after I told her I was not attending college. I then told her where I was from, and she responded, "Huntersville! Isn't that the neighborhood where all that stuff be happening?" After my response, the look on her face said it all. I felt like I didn't stand a chance. I was too hood for her daughter. Her mother gave me the third degree. She wrote down my license plate number and date of birth. She didn't stop there; she also wrote down my social security number. She then placed it on the refrigerator. Kellen's mom then went on to say, "My daughter has never been drunk or pregnant, and I expect her to come back that way." I had never met anyone like her in my life. I thought I was going out with the Antichrist's daughter! This was something new for me. I decided to act like I had some sense.

Kellen was attracted to me, but not just because of my good looks. I was one to go against the grain. I must admit that her mother had me shook, but I couldn't tell her that. The first time we went out, Kellen was trying to get me in trouble. She assumed that I was with it, but boy was she wrong! I had Kellen home fifteen minutes ahead of time. She was rebellious because her mother was very strict. It was supposed to be a fling, but I decided to hang around for a while. She was completely different from the young ladies on my side of the tracks. Her mother felt like I wasn't good enough for her daughter, and she didn't even know about my kids. Kellen and I were supposed to have a few laughs, and that's all. I had no intention of taking it this far. I introduced Kellen to Queshara, my youngest daughter. She was about three months old at the time. I couldn't let her meet Rachel, my oldest daughter, because I was barely seeing her myself. I was having baby momma drama! I was catching it from both ends. Queshara's mom and I still had some loose ends. I always said, "You can take the girl out of the hood, but you can't take the hood out of the girl." I guess I did kind of leave her hanging. Besides, we grew up in the same church, and she played a major part in my life in the beginning. She lived with me at my mother's house for a while. Although that didn't last long, I have to say she was my down chick. What do I mean by that? Survival by any means! I was broke, and she would give me her income tax money to flip. I would take her tax return and purchase a couple pounds of weed. She was already pregnant by someone else when we were kicking it. Unfortunately for her son, his dad was pulling some major time in prison. She was very jealous. I told her that I was being true to her, and I meant it. It was after I got tired of proving myself that I started doing what I do best. I lost face a long time ago; that honest part of me died with my grandmother. I ran out on that relationship just like everything else I started in life.

There I was, dating Kellen, with my kids' mothers on my coattails. With the pressure I had to handle at that time, it's a wonder I didn't smoke or drink. I also had quite a few women on the side. Kellen accepted me with all my flaws. She had no plans of dealing with me that long, but that small crush blossomed into something beautiful and ugly. Here we were, banging our heads against the wall trying to figure out a few things. When would be the best time to tell her mom? Out of nowhere, the unthinkable happened. Kellen and I had only been dating for a few months. Just when things were getting good, my daughter's mom pulled up with my daughter and about five chicken heads in the car. A chicken head is a woman with no aspirations; she's often loud for no reason, and she loves drama. More times than not, she's persistent and very intelligent when it comes to using the system for assistance. Extremely dangerous! My daughter's mother jumped out of the car screaming, trying to make me look bad. She blurted out "That's why you can't spend any time with your daughter; you're too busy spending time with that b**ch!" I begged Kellen to go into the house. It was a task, because she can be stubborn at times. She finally went into the house, and I attempted to leave her home; the last thing I needed was for her mother to have heard what was going on outside her front door. Her friends were laughing, and I was very upset! She tried to make it seem like I was a deadbeat dad. She was upset because I didn't want to have anything to do with her. This was just one of the results of my bad decision making. Sometimes you only get one shot at making the right decision. Shortly after this incident, I was happy to know I still had a chance with Kellen.

Moving on to my first love, music, I hooked up with Jason, also known as Second Sun. We eventually became roommates and good friends. He was attending Norfolk State University at the time, and I wanted to get out of my mother's house. We got an apartment together, a bachelor pad! He produced, and I wrote all of the lyrics. I started waking up and falling asleep writing. Between Jason, classes, and the streets, all we did was record music. We had a bootleg studio simply because we couldn't afford to be paying twenty-five dollars an hour to record. We improvised and took the top off of a record player. Next we placed a cheap microphone inside of it. We had to record at crazy hours because our microphone would pick up every little noise in the neighborhood, making our mix come out distorted. That didn't stop us. I began to take my music seriously, and so I recorded my first album in-house. I can't say that it had the best sound, but we felt like we were on to something.

I was still an apprentice at the shipyard in Newport News at the time. I was beginning to hate it. I used to sneak away from different job sites in order to write lyrics. It became so bad; I started failing some of my classes. I would drift off and write lyrics all day. I had no desire to be in school or work at the shipyard anymore. I figured that I could just sell dope and weed in order to record full-time. I pursued a not-likely-to-ever-happen career. I know: genius! I was placed on academic probation and given my first warning. That didn't wake me up at all. The only reason I was still going to work was because I needed a job on file for child support. I was making enough money in the streets to take care of my bills. All I had to pay was half of my rent, child support, and a car note. How hard is that? All I had to do was flip a couple of pounds a week. That was easier said than done, especially without the clientele. I was young, dumb, and ambitious for all the wrong reasons. I honestly thought that this was going to work out. I figured that the worst case scenario was that I could always set up a sting. I used to get close to my connections and take consignment. After I made them a couple of grand, they would get careless. You know what they say: "You should keep your fiends close, and enemies even closer." Those are words to live by. As soon as they let their guards down, I bucked on them. I figured I'd deal with the consequences later. I was like, "See you when I see you!" I hung around live wires, people without a care in the world. I even started turning tricks or, shall I say, "a favor for a favor." There was nothing these women wouldn't do for a little piece of what they called heaven. I took advantage of that. I would let somebody's mother, daughter, sister, or wife degrade herself. I use to enjoy looking down on them. It gave me a sense of control. On the flip side of that, I finally did it: I flunked out of school. The childhood mistakes had begun to turn into adulthood catastrophes. I got kicked out of school and lost a good job with benefits. I had two infants at the time, and I couldn't care less. I was traveling the same path that my father and brother had traveled.

Chapter 19
The Beginning

Jason and I stumbled across the perfect ingredients: beauty, attitude, and voice when Kellen introduced us to one of her good friends, Erica. I put her to work immediately after hearing her sing. She was the only female who spent as much time at the bachelor pad as I did. She had the sound and the looks. The sky was the limit, and we had plans to attain the stars. I had a lot more time to record because I was out of work. I was also out of school with no plans of going back. I was in love with the streets. Everything came second to money, even my freedom. The only thing remotely close was a woman. I kept at least six in rotation. I had it bad!

The life that appeared to be fabulous wasn't so fabulous, however; everyone around me started going to jail and getting killed. It was nothing to watch the news and hear about people getting killed. But it was different when you saw someone you grew up with on the channel 13 news because he or she was murdered. After seeing so many familiar faces disappear, I begin to re-examine myself. I wasn't much of a father at this time. I was more like the visiting uncle to my children. I felt like I was doing my job because I was taking care of them financially, but I was still considered a deadbeat dad. Child support was riding me hard, and the guys I ran with were disappearing fast. That didn't stop me from grinding. In and out of jobs, I brought my kids what I thought they needed. I stopped paying my child support, but at this time, I was only a couple of hundred dollars in debt with them. The police were trying to lock me up.

At this point in my life, I had attended Scared Straight, been kicked out of school, robbed, been robbed, and attended anger management. I was starting to feel like things just weren't ever going to be right. I knew I had to change, but I just didn't have a clue of where to begin. I was giving up on my music just like everything else. I told Jason and Erica that I had a few things I needed to take care of. It was too much trying to keep up with reality while chasing this dream. I was about to do the unthinkable. I was trying to run away from my problems instead of facing them. I attempted to join the military. I had some things I needed to take care of before I could leave, however. I felt rejected, as not even the military would accept me. The marines at that! They needed people, and I still was stuck. I was unable to run away from these problems, but little did I know my real problems were just around the corner. I took care of everything my recruiter told me I needed to take care of in order to join. This time I was going into the army instead of the marines. I just wanted to get away! I did everything I could do. It was just a matter of time, but when you're impatient, you make irrational decisions. I was still pushing my demo at the time. I had a few people interested in my sound, but they weren't saying anything I wanted to hear. I hooked up with Big Chief Entertainment. He said that we were about to do some big things. He loved my sound, but he was going to put a guy that went by the name of Big Guns Supreme out first. He said that he had an investor. It sounded good, but I knew that more than likely he couldn't do any more for me than I was doing for myself. He too was wishing upon a star.

Shortly after I met with this guy, I got into a brawl with a close family member. We shared the same blood and broke bread together in the streets. We were joined at the hip; when you saw me, you saw him. When money and women are involved, the story always ends the same way, sadly. We had an ugly dispute that resulted in a closed fist causing blood. Our grandmothers are probably turning in their graves right now. He allowed himself to get sucked in, and he became just like the rest of those disrespectful bastards. Every time somebody robbed him, guess whom he came running to? He decided that he would act stupid and so I confronted him about it. Just like I expected, he tried to play hard in front of his new friends. I had to pull his head out of the clouds and bring him back to reality. I must admit, I was hurt. All love was lost, and a lifetime friendship would end over money and drugs. I knew that the best way to hurt him was to hit his pockets.

Meanwhile, I had failed at something else. I couldn't even sell dope to stay on top. My stomach was touching my back, and I was open to any means of getting money. Blood was no longer thicker then water. Prior to this incident, I had made a commitment to Kellen. I was asked to escort her to her debutant ball, and we had been preparing for this event for a couple of months. Once again, I was to let her down. Failure had become routine for me. The day of the ball the unthinkable happened. As a result, I ended up in jail. Now let's pick up from the top of this story. How did I get here? I asked myself that over and over again. How did my life play out that way? Earlier that morning, I was on my way to the barbershop. I just so happened to run into one of many mischievous people. He said something that was like music to my ears. You know that little problem I had? Remember I said, "The best way to hurt him was to hit his pockets"? Well, I began to salivate from the mouth as if a juicy steak were lying on a platter before me. Let's just say the Devil has a way of playing off of our weaknesses. Everything this cat was saying appealed to my innermost lustful deliberations. I was too busy thinking about myself, as usual. Knowing that all actions have consequences, I still wasn't smart enough to walk away. Once the crime was committed, I took off running. I must admit that like never before, I had once again placed my hand in the cookie jar. My thoughts were scrambled, my breathing was irregular, and my heart began beating as if it were about to explode from my chest. A million things were going through my mind at once. My thoughts were clashing. Everything was going wrong at this point in my life. I acted off impulse; my actions were nothing short of reckless. Unfortunately, there is cause and effect, consequences and repercussions. I tried to change the outcome, but the deed was done. I had a change of heart a little too late. It happened so fast! I dropped my head in despair. Once I raised my head, I was in the back of a patrol car, and my risk was bounded by handcuffs. I ended up being booked, processed, and interrogated. I had something on me when I was taken into custody that could have imprisoned me for a long time. The Lord was not ready for me yet. After strip-searching me, they didn't find anything. I was not only being stripped by the law, but I was also being stripped by the Lord. The object that could have imprisoned me positioned itself within the material I was wearing. I was not lucky; I was blessed! I could feel the evidence on me, but they never found it. I was scared to use the restroom because there was a chance I would pry it loose. I held on to the evidence until I got bonded out later that night.

I had a completely different perspective on life after that incident. I realized that God had spared my life and given me a second chance. After escaping the grasp of confinement, even poverty didn't seem so bad. I still was hardheaded, but I was not as quick to make a move without thought. I still had to appear before the court and face the music. They say you're innocent until proven guilty. This would be logical to someone who never had the opportunity to foxtrot with the system. I still say, "You're guilty until proven innocent." My recruiter called me on that following Monday to give me some good news. This is what being impatient gets you. Patience is a virtue, and life is like a game of chess, you must think before you move. Did I fail to mention that I had already signed a contract and sworn in the first time? My recruiter was calling me to tell me that the job I wanted was available, and I would be stationed; she would pick me up and take me to Richmond, Virginia. All I had to do was swear in one more time, and I was off to boot camp. Only I knew that I was doing this to just get away! I didn't really want to join the military. No matter where they sent me in this world, I couldn't leave myself behind. I told her I appreciated the good news but that I had some bad news.

"What's wrong, Johnta?" she asked. "You had to fix so much to get to this point, and you waited for so long. What could you have possibly done to throw all that hard work out the window? God will test you on your journey to success. Not because he wants you to fail, but because he wants to make sure you're strong once you get there." I told her what had happened, and I asked her if she would testify on my behalf. She agreed to. The arresting officer also testified on my behalf. Imagine someone you played sports with in high school arresting you for a crime such as this. I was so embarrassed. I was arrested three times from one incident. Every time I went to court, they brought new charges against me. I was stressed out and broke. I had no idea where my life was heading. I knew I was traveling an obscure path, but when you surround yourself with pessimism, what do you expect? I was traveling through life without care. I didn't enjoy the view; most people don't. You find yourself too busy worrying about what you don't have instead of appreciating what you do have. Needless to say, Kellen hung in there with me. She was at every court case, and she also gave me some of her scholarship money to assist with the lawyer fees. She used her mother's car to take me to work once my car had been repossessed. On the verge of losing my apartment, my roommate, Jason proved to be a great friend. He gave me $500 to give to my attorney. This was some of his refund money from financial aid.

Recognize every blessing. See how God works in mysterious ways. It was written; he already had the army I needed to win this battle set in place. God is good all of the time. Jason also paid my half of the rent for that month. We eventually lost our apartment, and I ended up back home with my mother. This was a reality check for me. I found out who my real friends were, and I realized that some people aren't placed in your life by coincidence. I committed that crime, and I walked out of that court room a liar. I raised my right hand and swore to tell the truth, but I saw my entire life flash before my eyes. I asked myself, "Is this how my brother felt just before his entire life changed?" He was right when he said, "You don't want to come in here." So I did what I used to do best, I lied! The Lord knew it and so did I, but he allowed me to bear witness to every man who is thinking about doing something stupid and to any man who is thinking about ruining someone else's life as well as his own. (**No problem is too big or too small for God.**)

I had so much on my plate, and Kellen was over three hundred miles away. I could have called a number of women in the tidewater area, but instead I drove to Blacksburg, Virginia in the middle of the night just to lay my head on her lap. I just needed to hear her voice and place within my nose that natural sweet scent of her. I just needed to hear her say everything was going to be all right. It was then I realized that I had to have her in my life. She wrapped my mind with peace that morning. Two lawyers, three charges, and six months later, it was time for judgment day. I was ready for whatever was coming my way. My destiny was not in the hands of this judge, but in the hands of God.

"Mr. Knight, would you like to say anything on your behalf?"

I took a deep breath and went on to say, "I have been arrested three times for the same incident. Every time I come to court, I'm told to turn myself in. It's impossible for me to make plans for my future if I'm not sure where I'm going. I would appreciate it if you made a decision today, sir. I don't mean any disrespect, but I'm ready to get on with my life."

Shortly after the judge reached his decision, he said, "I find the defendant ..."

At that moment, I stopped breathing. It was as if time had come to a standstill. The judge went on to say, "not guilty!" I was found not guilty of both felony charges, but I had to eat the misdemeanor charge. I didn't care, because I was going home. I was given a second chance at life. The judge told me he didn't want to ever see my face again, and he wished me luck with my military career. My family had doubts, and they had every reason to. They still hung in there with me despite all their qualms. I'll always love them for that! I made it over another obstacle in my life. I had every intention from that day forward to do the right thing. Why did I feel no joy? I'll tell you why: the decision was unjust. I didn't deserve to inhale freedom and exhale victory. I was free to leave the courtroom, yet I was in no rush. It was if my feet had transformed into roots planted in soil. I wanted to scream out, "I'm guilty!" I reeked with culpability.

Now I have to bear witness to what God has done for me. How he loves us even when we do not deserve it. I hear you, Lord; I hear you loud and clear. Shortly after my final case, I had to report to Richmond, Virginia. I was to become property of Uncle Sam. I had to make a critical decision once I arrived there. I could tell the truth and get disqualified like so many times before, or I could take my chances and stretch out the truth. I put in a lot of work to get there. I didn't want to throw it all away. I should have thought about all of that before. God forgives, but you have to forgive yourself for things you've done in the past in order to move forward. I decided to tell the truth, to try something different for a change. I had to get up at four in the morning. Although I had just finished explaining myself to the judge, I still owed the military justification. Over to the down town federal building I went! This was one of the longest unproductive days of my life. How could someone spend an entire day backpedaling? I'll tell you how. I was a master at screwing up. I arrived there around five in the morning, and I had to wait until four that evening before they called me in. I had to explain why I was unable to leave on my departure date. I stayed up there until seven that night. It took about twelve hours to find out I could no longer join. I was disqualified, and I received a dishonorable discharge before I even got my career started. I also lied to keep my recruiter from getting into trouble. Someone has to die in order for someone to live. Let's just say a recruiter's job is to get you in by any means necessary. I must say, "I love my country!" Home of the slaves, land of the greedy! I told them that I concealed information from my recruiter. There was no need to mess up her career. I left the downtown federal building for the last time. A few hours later, I was back in the jungle.

Chapter 20
What's Next?

I had no idea of what I was going to do with my life, but I had to think of something fast. When you have children to feed, you have to take the first thing available. I was now about three thousand dollars behind on my child support. It was only getting worse. When I was a kid, it was always a black and white thing. The way some of my relatives spoke, I thought that all white people were evil. You know that phrase, "working for the man." The man could be male or female, but the man was always white. I had to come into my own before I realized that there will always be ignorant people out here, but it had nothing to do with race and everything to do with character. The Lord put another wonderful person in my life, and she was Caucasian. I met Kay shortly before I was going into the military. I began working for her prior to my attempt to join. What made this relationship so special was that it was a classic example of two people heavily depending on each other. The first time she hired me, I quit on her. I remember she took me to see this jacked up account I was suppose to clean for her; I didn't last eight hours. This might have been new to her, but not for me. I had developed a pattern, a routine of giving up on everything. Whenever times got tough, I would always locate the exit. Kay was a franchise owner for a cleaning service. An older Caucasian woman with a very big heart, she hired me and trusted me. Although I told her why I didn't get into the military, she didn't look at me like some young black criminal she couldn't trust. Yes, I did quit on her the first time when she needed me, but she still gave me a second chance. I helped her get her business off the ground, and in return, she made me a responsible and dependable young man. I was very appreciative of this second opportunity, regardless of what it was. I became the best custodian ever.

The Lord works in mysterious ways, and for the first time, I would recognize one of his many blessings. You might want a Benz, but the Lord won't give it to you; he'll give you transportation and a job. It's up to you to get in that car that you don't like and go to work every day. It's up to you to work hard and earn that Benz. Prayer can't replace effort, and effort can't replace prayer. I said all of this to express that it's not about what you're doing in life; it's about taking advantage of any and every opportunity in order to get to where you want to be in life. I like to call those chains of opportunities "stepping stones." I started off working one shift, and then I ended up working everyone else's accounts, too. I was tired but very grateful. I wanted to quit many times! But I thought about how much Kay had done for me, not financially, but how she helped me build good character. I thought about my kids, my future with Kellen, and how blessed I was to be working. After all, I could have been working for the state with numbers on my back for pennies.

Even though I worked all the time, I still was struggling to pay my current support. My arrears kept accumulating interest. About two years later, my arrears' total was about $8,000. Every time I went to court, they gave me a certain amount I had to pay on that day, or I would be incarcerated. It seemed as if I was going to jail one way or another. I had to come up with the money in order to stay out of jail. Kay gave me loans on top of my income. At one point, it felt as if I was working for free, and I had to take on more work in order to stay afloat. I barely slept, and because of my stress, I needed an outlet. So I got back into doing music again. Music was the only thing keeping me sane, my anti-drug. I got very frustrated with my situation, but things seem to always get worse before they get better. My producer Jason ended up getting married and moving to Germany. On top of that, I lost an entire book of lyrics. The one guy who could take my art and tailor fit a beat to my lyrics was putting the music aside. I guess this is how it feels when you give up on people. It's a bitter taste, a reality check to yourself. I had given up on countless people; it hurts!

I was later introduced to another producer by the name of Jon Vegas.

This was around the same time I met Everett. Everett was working in the same building I was cleaning full-time. This was my main account. He heard about me from none other than Big Chief Entertainment, the ghetto governor. Remember when I said he was going to put me on the back burner for Big Guns Supreme? Well, that didn't happen. Everett asked me if I had a demo, so I went and got it. I was supposed to be part of Big Chief Entertainment, but he had only let Everett hear Big Guns Supreme's demo. Evidently he didn't care about the better music; he was looking out for a friend. After Everett heard my demo, he cut Big Chief off. When he told them why, they called me. I tried to be fair. I said, "Everett has about five thousand that he's willing to put in this project. How about we split it?"

Their response was, "We'll get to you after we push Guns Supreme's project."

"Good luck with that!" I said.

I introduced Everett to Erica, and he was sold on the whole idea of Multi-stylez and Ices for our stage names. I didn't have to record out of another bootleg studio. It was on! I wrote all of the material for us. We recorded at several different studios: Street Rats Productions, Third Eye Entertainment, Millennium, etc. … I was now about to start recording at Fast Tracks, which was only a few miles from Everett's house. Mike Unique was the studio engineer, and I really liked his work. He put a lot into my project, and it turned out great. Chris was the owner at the time, and he took care of the graphics. His work was incredible, and I was excited. I had vinyl for the DJs, posters, postcards, and CDs. I had been through a lot, or, shall I say, I put myself through a lot. Nevertheless, I was beginning to see some light at the end of the tunnel. I still had a long way to go, but I was a lot further than I would have ever imagined. To this day, I appreciate everything that Everett has done for me. He believed in my project just as much as I did. He introduced Erica and me to one of his partners in New York, Tyrone. He looked just like Big Red from the movie *The Five Heartbeats*, saying, "My hours are from nine to five." He was a very persistent dude. He kept us very busy, in fact. He took very good care of us. Every weekend he had some hole-in-the-wall venue set up for us. We didn't care where we performed; we just wanted to be on stage. We were ecstatic about performing in the Big Apple. That's all that mattered to us. We could care less when or where. Jamaica Queens was where we laid our heads, but Harlem and Manhattan were where we performed. We also made our way out to Jersey. I thought, *I was made for this!* Every Friday night after work, I would hit route 13 heading north, making my way to the big city. I was what you would label a starving artist. Nothing else mattered. If you don't believe in yourself, who will? I drove off of octane fumes without any money just to perform for a few minutes in a city six hours away. Then I would turn around and drive six hours back at the end of my performance. This is what we call passion, and passion is something you absolutely must have. I can recall one of my cars breaking down in Time Square. How embarrassing is that? I also took my chances with a car with no heat, air conditioning, or radio. I had to listen to the wind for six hours traveling north and six hours traveling back.

But just like everything else in my life, when things didn't move fast enough, I quit. I quit on everyone. I fell from the music scene for another four years. Everything had been moving slowly, but it was at least going. Music had been the only stable thing in my life at that point, and I even quit on that. I had a problem! I stopped caring and started feeling sorry for myself. What's the point? This is how simple it is to accept failure; if you're not careful, it will weigh you down. I fell into a deep depression. I started having an identity crisis. *Who are you?* I've been asking myself this question for years. *If you don't know who you are, how can you possibly move forward in life?* Standing in front of a crowd and behind a microphone was all I really knew. Without the music, I no longer had a pulse. Flat line ….

Chapter 21
Recognizing Your Blessings

I began to walk around as if I were in prison, confined to my own frame. I started acting out like the world owed me something. I had to get a grip, and fast! So what if I didn't make the pros, or get a record deal? I still had my kids and Kellen. I had a loving family, my sisters, and a wonderful mother. I'm blessed, and I don't even act like it. The Lord was still in my corner with all my faults. It's a fixed fight! I still didn't favor him, and I eventually paid the price. Are you familiar with the saying, "The Lord giveth and the Lord taketh away"? Those are words to live by; I can bear witness to that. I was blessed with a job in which I made twenty dollars an hour, along with good benefits and a 401(k) plan. This blessing had me working around seventy hours a week. Some people barely worked forty hours. Many people where getting laid off. I was beat down by the system, but things were about to change. In just eight months, I was able to pay off my nine thousand dollar child support debt. That was like lifting a bolder from my chest. I still ignored this blessing like so many others. I was egocentric! You can't put the Lord first if you're selfish.

In spite of my actions, he continued to work in my favor. Blessing number two would come with a huge bow on top. Never in a million years did I expect what would come next. Viewed as a deadbeat dad on paper, I finally got an opportunity to step up to the plate. My oldest daughter's mom dropped the ball. I picked it up and never looked back. She treated me like crap. In order to see my daughter, I had to deal with it. I felt no need to fight her in court because the system is biased with regard to gender. Who was I? Up until that point, they hadn't treated me any different from every other man I'd seen get his butt handed to him in court. One thing I did know was that you can't win a battle if you don't fight. I can recall paying it forward. My grandmother used to say, "God don't like ugly!" After all that my daughter's mom did to me, I was in a perfect position to return the favor. After all of the accusations and humiliation in court, it was coming full circle. If I were ever a dollar short on my child support, she wouldn't open the door. I ended up with custody of my oldest daughter, and not long after, I received custody of my youngest daughter. Tell me my God isn't a favorable one! After all he had done for me, I had never said, "Thank you, Jesus." This was just the beginning of a long and tiring battle. Still, in and out of court, I fought to keep my girls. I had help from my mother; I can't even begin to express what that woman has done for me.

During this time, Kellen was a senior at Virginia Tech University. I was still doing dirt on top of dirt, although I was being blessed continuously. It was still sort of about me. The girls slowed me down, but they never brought me to a complete halt. How could I speak badly about a man I was becoming—my father? I had become a womanizer, and I would go on to struggle with it for years to come. I had to learn how to cook, clean, and make an attempt to do hair. My efforts did not go unnoticed. Their kindergarten teacher, among many other women, thought it was cute. A man raising two girls … I was on another level. Guys wanted to know how I went about getting custody, and women had other intentions. I took advantage of every opportunity that presented itself. I ended up sleeping with my daughter's teacher. I was wrong for this one. I didn't deserve Kellen, but regardless of what she knew or assumed, she loved me hard. I couldn't imagine how she felt, and I almost didn't care until someone stuck their hand in my cookie jar. Tables would turn; she finally had enough. After receiving a dose of my own medicine, I was crushed. I couldn't get this off my mind for years. The reality of my Kellen being with someone else almost killed me. I guess this is what it feels like. She forgave me; why couldn't I forgive her? I loved her and disliked her all at the same time. I placed her on a pedestal, and no matter what I did, I couldn't imagine her dropping to my level. She forgave me a million times, but this incident alone crushed my ego. Vindictive woman, she paid me back a million times with one lethal blow. Instead of it teaching me a lesson, it made me worse. I was without feeling and had very little conscience.

In the midst of all this, I managed to get another female pregnant. I had yet another problem. Oh, how my infidelities continue to come back to haunt me. Can things get any worse? Never ask that question. I knew for sure after the results came back that the baby would be mine. Kellen and I would be no more. I found out about my son when he was three months old. My son's mother and I were just cool. She was someone I kicked it with a couple of times, nothing more. I stopped by to say hi, and her mother just so happened to hear her mention my name. She made her way from the back of the house, and she said, "So you're Johnta!"

"Yes, I am."

I didn't think anything of it until she said, "Say hello to your son."

That's how I found out about my third child; that made baby number three.

At the time, Kellen was living with her father. She had recently graduated from college. Prior to this incident, I told her that I really needed her. Can you believe I had the nerve to ask for her help? I told her that my girls were struggling in school, and I was working way too much. She stepped up to the plate; now that's unconditional love. We moved into a townhouse, and she still wanted to marry me with all my flaws. With all that had taken place, I still didn't recognize my blessings. I proposed to her, and she said yes. My reasons for getting married weren't good at all. I really wasn't ready, but I was afraid of losing her; so once again, I made it more about me. We had a beautiful big wedding, spent a lot of money, and I still was ungrateful. Compared to everything I'd been through, I was still on top, but I didn't see it that way. Not long after being married, discrepancies would rain. The Lord giveth and the Lord taketh away! I lost my job. The improbable happened! The Ford plant shut down. Kellen was not making much money, and I had no idea what my next move would be.

Chapter 22
Grandma Was Right

Just married, out of a job, and broke; what a way to start a life journey with someone! This is the part of life where you separate the boys from the men. What next? It felt as if I were playing the quarterback position like I once did, except this was far from any game. I could make bad decisions on the field and make up for it on the next play, but life does not work out that way. I compare the field to reality because I've had to make critical decisions under pressure. I felt like a three-hundred-pound lineman had sacked me from my blind side. I never saw this one coming. I just said, "I do." I didn't even have an income. How do you accept going from bringing close to a thousand dollars a week home to only three hundred in unemployment checks? The same expenses applied, but I didn't have the funds to keep up. One thing that applies in life and on the field is that you must "never let them see you sweat!"

When the quarterback sweats, so does the team. I'm playing a similar position in life; if the head of the household panics, so does the family. The sun would shine on the outside, but heavy dark clouds shadowed happiness from within. I bear witness to the saying, "When it rains, it pours." I panicked, but I couldn't show it. I refused to show my wife or my kids any signs of weakness. This was no longer all about me. The decisions I made from then on affected everyone.

I was blessed with a job less than a month after being laid off. I was making nowhere close to what I had been making at Johnson Control. My money was so short. I ended up having to pay the Virginia Employment Commission back because I had continued to receive checks while employed. I thought to myself, "One more check won't hurt." Under no circumstances can you make right from wrong. Like grandma said, "The Lord doesn't like ugly." This would be a reality check; life was screaming out, "So what are you going to do?" I had become accustomed to slipping through the cracks, but not this time. I'd finally hit a wall of problems and had no solution. But when times get tight, you do whatever you have to do to get by. When you have a hustler's mentality, you make life bearable. Believe me when I tell you that ten times out of ten, you will resort to what you know. As soon as I tried to push again, I quickly realized that I was no longer that person anymore. Who was I?

Grandma was right! She said that I would come back willingly or on my knees. I have to say that Jesus broke me down. Instead of distributing crack or weed, I got back into church. Unfortunately, I nearly depleted my 401(k) just to keep our heads above water. I now look at the glass as half full instead of half empty. I recognize even the smallest blessing now. At least I had it to spend. I took a seven-dollar pay cut, but at least I was working. Grandma was always right, and I was thankful for what I had. Thank the Lord for my Dorothy Mae; my big momma!

Chapter 23
Closure after Seventeen Years

His reentry in my life was somewhat peculiar. I had not at this point seen my father since I was kid. Now that I was a man like him, the guy I knew as Dad wore an imperceptible face. My old man and I would finally put that chapter behind us. We would attempt to close for once an interval that could only get wider in time. This was a conversation way overdue! I didn't take the road less traveled; I decided to follow my father's footsteps. The signs where there, but just like him, I chose a somewhat vague path. Should he be fought? The answer to that question is, to some extent, two-parted. If I turned out to be so much like him, although he wasn't in attendance for quite some time, could I argue the point that I didn't have a choice? That it was "in my blood"? Do I really have an argument when I say it's genetics, or do I have excuses like so many others before me? The first response could be without thought, simply yes. It is just excuses! My second response could be viewed in several different ways. Instead of leaving me to play detective and follow his footsteps, he could have stayed involved and told me to be more attentive to the signs. The signs were there, but my maturity was nonexistent.

Notice that I'm not blaming it on my background or race but on my lack of parental guidance. He knew exactly where this road I was traveling would end. In order to know what is going on in a child's life, you have to be involved in it. As I said, the guy I once knew as Dad wore a strange face. This was an uncomfortable moment for both of us. Shame hovered over his head, and he couldn't even look at me. I wanted to say something, but I was without words. I thought to myself, *Do I call him Dad or address him as I would any other stranger?* He began to speak, but I only saw his lips moving, because I was so angry. So much time had passed, and to try to rekindle what we once had was of no interest to me. I never said I didn't love my father, but I felt betrayed. How could someone walk out on someone he loves? I thought to myself, *I'm your flesh and blood; your son!* How dare he leave me without chance? He knew how harsh reality could be. Did he not love me enough to care? Did his decision go without thought? All I knew at that point was that he left me to charter deep waters, and therefore the gap between us would remain.

A few years passed, and I continued to keep him at arm's length. I had become just like him, deceitful and egotistic. They say the fruit does not fall far from the tree. Time would begin to beat me down, as it did him. Slowly but surely, by the time I turned twenty-seven, I would find myself without guards. I stopped playing the defensive and decided to let my dad in. We started hanging out more. I found myself enjoying his company a lot. This was more than two guys chilling; this was a kid and his father. The kid from within was reaching for that attention he'd so desperately needed all of those years. Here it was, seventeen years later, and I was just realizing how much I'd missed my dad. The hatred I'd once felt for him was replaced by the love that had been misplaced but always there. The relationship that had been strained was healing nicely. I told him that I forgave him for the decisions he made and, more importantly, that I understood. If I had not walked the same path, I would not have ever been able to understand. I would not have been able to forgive him. Until we let go of the past, we will never move forward. Neither of us felt well about the decisions we had made in our past. We chose to take steps toward a righteous future together. Had I not chosen to take the same route as he, I probably would not have arrived at forgiveness. Father Time has no intention of turning back, and neither do I. There's no sense in crying over spilled milk.

There I was, twenty-nine years old, and I was beginning to find more pieces to the puzzle of life. My brother still carries somewhat of a burden, but when the three of us are together, you would think we were the best of friends. Despite that brutal road my brother had to travel, he turned out to be a pretty good person. After thirteen years in a correctional facility, my brother came home and did the complete opposite of what was expected of him. I commend him for that. I still look up to my big brother despite his past. I'm far from a saint myself. He still resides in a cynical environment, but he now has a son of his own.

One thing Dad taught us is how not to be a man. To make a long story short, I love those guys! I think all three of us are trying to figure out the man in the glass. When you get what you want in your struggle for yourself and the world makes you king for a day, just go to the mirror, look at yourself, and see what the man there has to say. People will always judge you—especially those closest to you. At the end of the day, if you can't look at yourself in the mirror and say to that man, "I'm proud of you," then everyone else's opinion won't matter. For it isn't your father, mother, or wife upon whose judgment you must pass. The fellow whose verdict counts most in your life is the one staring back from the glass.

PART 3

Transitioning from a Boy to a Man: The Spiritual Realm

Chapter 24
Entering the Spiritual Realm

There's not a single word in the entire *Merriam-Webster Dictionary* to sum up the woman I married. Kellen Knight is my backbone, and no one including myself can understand why she married me. She's an extraordinary woman! She really does have superpowers—seriously. Any woman who can take on three children who are not hers, those three kids' mothers, and a deceitful husband, deserves the world. The way she looks at me when she says, "I love you," sends chills down my spine. The way she cups my face with her hands when she says, "You're so good to me," brings tears to the rim of my eyes. At night, her body language silently speaks aloud. It says, "I'm safe here in your arms." She stood the test of time, regardless of how her family members and friends felt about me. I'm no longer that man I once was. You can lead a horse to water, but you can't make him drink. No one changes unless he wants to change. I've decided to put God first. As a result of this change, we're so much happier. The job I once hated doesn't seem so bad anymore. I've arrived, and I still have the girl. I have a favorable God, and I urge you to try him out. Let go, and let God. I asked him to take that urge for different women away from me, and he did just that. As long as I'm in the flesh, this will always be a battle. But remember, the battle is not yours; it's the Lord's. Change can't happen without effort. I no longer have to ask the question, "Who am I?" I know who I am. My wife said she stayed with me not only because she loved me, but also because she saw potential in me. The Lord works in mysterious ways! I took a pay cut, and she got a raise. Then she got fired from a job that she hated so much she would come home crying. I told her not to worry; I'd take care of us. The pastor said sometimes the Lord places you in the eye of a hurricane just so you will end up in the right direction. She was up when I was down, and I return the favor. I'm her crutch, and she's mine. I love my wife so much! People often say that the Lord saved them, but I like to say, "My wife saved me from myself and the Lord delivered me!"

Chapter 25
Bondage Begins with You

Conforming to the ways of the world would be your first step in bondage. Galatians 5:1 says not to let anything or anyone hold you in bondage, "but stand fast therefore in the liberty wherewith Christ hath made you free."(KJV) You have to jump-start your spiritual metabolism. You have to truly believe in Christ. I could not care less about your denomination. We have to commit ourselves to spreading the good news (the Word). John 1:1, 5 says, "In the beginning was the word and the word was with God … The light shines in the darkness, and the darkness can never extinguish it" (NLT). You see, we were never supposed to take part in the ways of the world. All of the hardship I encountered mostly came from me pursuing the world. I'm far from perfect, and I would be the first to admit that now. But at one point in my life, you couldn't tell me anything. My mind was made up! The pleasures of the world were so much more fulfilling than some unrealistic commandments. How can a man be held accountable for anything in this day and time? It was that way of thinking that almost got me killed on several occasions. That way of thinking almost cost me my wife, family, and friends. Overextending yourself is a form of bondage. Accumulating unnecessary bills is a form of bondage. Trying to live beyond your means is a form of bondage. There are so many ways you can be in bondage when you attempt to take on the weight of the world. No one in the flesh is strong enough to do that.

I had no idea that life could be so beautiful until I began my journey by faith. Call on Christ and free yourself! Once you do this, your mind will be renewed, and your strength will be restored. Just like a baby, you will have to learn how to walk all over again, because walking with Jesus requires a strong set of legs. Are you living or just waiting to die? What I mean by this is are you enjoying your life here on earth? You should store your treasures for heaven, but while you are here on earth, you shouldn't put yourself in any predicament that causes you to be miserable from the weight of the world. Will you check out without knowing your purpose in life? Remember, a man without Christ is a lost man. One more thing, don't forget that prayer does not replace effort, and effort does not replace prayer. You have to have them both in order to progress. Keep God first!

Chapter 26
The Two Cs

Here are my questions about the two Cs! In which do you take comfort, cash or Christ? Deuteronomy 31:8 says, "The Lord himself goes before you and will be with you; he will never leave you nor forsake you. Do not be afraid; do not be discouraged" (NIV). Here the Lord assures you that you can take refuge in him. He's telling us not to worry, because he will protect us. Hebrew 13:5 says, "Keep your lives free from the love of money, and be content with what you have" (NIV). Are you familiar with the song titled, "For the Love of Money"? This song talks about the extents people would go to in order to have money. For the love of money, people will rob, steal, and kill. So sad, but so true! If we crave it so much with our sanity, imagine what we'll do to get it when our judgment has been impaired. The world is set up so that everything revolves around money. Whenever I broke into someone's home, I was looking for money or something I could get money for. When I sold drugs, I didn't do it to help someone with her addiction; I did it for money. Although I loved clothes and women, I needed money to get either or both. The Lord didn't say to hate money; he said not to love it. If you don't remember anything else, remember that money comes and goes! If you're not careful, your mind will go with it. So be careful in what you take comfort in.

Chapter 27
It Was a Mistake

No one man or woman here on earth has been or will ever be perfect in the flesh. A mistake, in my opinion, happens when you attempt to do the right things, but things just don't turn out the way you planned. But when you do something that you know is wrong and call it a mistake because it didn't go the way you planned, that's called reaping what you sow! For example, when I found out about my first child, I tried to play it cool, although I was terrified. I made that decision to lay with a woman out of wedlock, knowing I was wrong. You know what I said for many years? It was a mistake! It's never a mistake when you intentionally do something. You don't even regret your wrongdoing the majority of the time; you regret getting caught. My children were never a mistake, nor were my actions, because I was never intending to do anything right. My children didn't ask to be here out of wedlock. I didn't make a mistake, because my intentions were wrong from the beginning.

When you are unhealthy in the spiritual realm, you are subject to end up in unconstructive situations. My father lacked the knowledge of Christ, and this was a man just like the ones I chose to emulate. My father and uncles chose the world over the Word, and I followed them off the same cliff. When you're sick, you seek advice from a doctor. The majority of us seek help from someone who's suffering from the same disease, the world! You have to coexist in the world, but you most certainly don't have to take part in its evil ways. I had to be healed of this disease before I could help someone else recover. I now realize that a blind man who seeks Christ and walks by faith can truly see. But a boy who calls himself a man but just pursues the world and walks by sight is truly blind.

Chapter 28
True Success

What do I consider true success? I can tell you that my perception of true success has changed several times in the past ten years. Anyone's answer would depend on where he was in that point in his life. Your answer would also depend on where you are morally and your level of maturity. Striving to overachieve in the world and so often underachieving in Christ, in my case, resulted in premature success. Underdeveloped success is only an appetizer. This always leaves you craving for more. It wasn't until I became a God-fearing man that I got the chance to view more of the menu. My family and I will be eating well as long as I stay the course. In my opinion, true success is when mind, body, and soul are in accord. When you are healthy in all three areas, I would say that you are at least in the starter blocks. Trying is doing! So don't allow another moment to pass before you are on your mark, studying the Word, praying to get set, and seeking knowledge by asking God where and when to go.

Chapter 29
Get Connected! Stay Connected!

No one man or woman here on earth has been or ever will be perfect in the flesh. You can't be physically fit and spiritually unhealthy. I had to learn that the hard way. You have to jump-start your physical metabolism in order to see results. You consume good foods, work out, and burn off negative calories in order to get positive results. The more you do this, the more exercise you want to do. Now that you have created good eating habits, you've noticed that the unwanted weight has dropped. The same process has to take place in order to jump-start your spiritual metabolism and drop the negative weight of the world. You have to study and fellowship. You have to seek knowledge and pray for understanding. Remember that getting connected is easy; the Lord keeps his line open 24–7 for all. You have to also understand that instant gratification does not exist. So, my advice to you would be to get connected before it's too late. But once you get connected, I encourage you to stay connected. In order to do this, you must be obedient and resistant to the flesh and all of the impurities it loves. All my help comes from the Lord; if I can change, anyone with breath in his body can change. But you have to want to change! Having your father's mannerisms is genetics, but just because you have made bad decisions like your father doesn't mean those decisions are in your blood; you just made bad decisions because you wanted to. So don't blame it on the generational curse; blame your own actions. If you point the finger at everyone but yourself, you're only making excuses.

and four out of five wonderful children. I teach all of my children about God first. I explain to them why the Bible is their shield against this evil world. I have two boys, and three girls to guide and teach. I don't want my daughters to settle for the man I was, and I don't want my sons to become the man I use to be. I've come a long way from what I was, and I will continue to strive to be the man the Lord wants me to be. I share my testimony with hopes to bring awareness to the youth, and older men like my father. Maybe some would seek knowledge, and maybe a few will change. It's time!